Wine, Food & the Arts: Works Gathered by
The American Institute of Wine & Food

Volume 1

Wine, Food & the Arts: Works Gathered by
The American Institute of Wine & Food

Published by The American Institute of Wine & Food

1550 Bryant Street, Suite 700, San Francisco, California 94103

Tel: 415-255-3000 Fax: 415-255-2874

The AIWF is a nonprofit organization incorporated in the state of California
for the purpose of encouraging scholarship and fostering
research in the study of wine and food.

This work was created by Swans Island Books in collaboration with
Madeleine Corson Design, San Francisco, California

Swans Island Books

One Edgewater Road

Belvedere, California 94920

Art archival research by Carousel Research, Inc.,
New York, New York

Printed in Hong Kong through Mandarin Offset

Giuseppe Arcimboldo, Autumn, frontispiece

Bartolomeo Bimbi, Grapes of 38 Varieties, x–xi

Wine, Food & the Arts

Works Gathered by

The American Institute

of Wine & Food

Introduction by Julia Child

VOLUME ONE

INTRODUCTION

This beautiful volume is the inaugural issue of our new annual, *Wine, Food & the Arts.* Since the founding of The AIWF in 1981, it has always been our goal to celebrate gastronomy not only through vigorous consumption, but most certainly in the form of the written word. Indeed, *The Journal of Gastronomy* did just that in its short and sporadic – but distinguished – life. Now, with art and articles gathered by The American Institute of Wine & Food, *The Journal* is transformed into the more permanent and infinitely more timely annual that you are now holding in your hands. | Much has happened gastronomically in this country during the last dozen or so years since The AIWF came into being. California wines already gaining prominence then are now accepted as world class. Furthermore, it is not only California that is producing wines: Grapes are being grown and harvested in almost every state in the union. Because of popular demand, American fresh produce has taken great steps forward, as is plainly evident when you compare our supermarkets now with the fruits and vegetables available to us 20 years ago. Of course, this is not true in all of this vast and diverse country, but the trend is moving forward. In addition, farmers' markets are appearing in many cities and small farmers are increasingly growing fruits, vegetables and herbs to satisfy the exacting needs of specialty markets, fine restaurants and innovative chefs.

While wine and wine growers have always had a certain privileged position in the public mind, those in the food professions used to be considered purely artisanal. At last, careers in the culinary arts have become respectable. Several of our excellent professional culinary schools are offering four-year bachelor's degrees in the liberal arts with a specialty in gastronomy, and we at last have a master's degree program at Boston University, the first ever offered anywhere. Because the culinary arts now have status, you will find students in their 30's and 40's who, discouraged by working at jobs that do not satisfy them, are leaving well-paid careers in other areas for careers in food and wine. The increasing presence of well-educated bakers, pastry chefs and *chefs de cuisine* in the kitchens of America is bringing real creativity and imagination to everything they touch. Writing beautifully and entertainingly about wine and food is certainly one of the fine arts. With the emergence of gastronomy as history and its acceptance as a totally absorbing and highly desirable discipline, we can expect to see ever more examples of fine writing and vivid illustration selected by our AIWF editors for succeeding annual volumes of *Wine, Food & the Arts.* ~ JULIA CHILD

To read about wine and food, to look at images of grapes and eggs and onions and pears, excites the tastebuds of our imagination as if we were drinking real wine and eating real food. We taste words, we savor images, with the same sensuous pleasure we take in opening an oyster and eating the sea. The primal arts of wine and food, of fermenting, cooking, drinking and eating — these are the arts that shape our senses and mold the poets and painters that load imaginary tables with real feasts. Since art is a communal table freed from time and place, we've considered the world our oyster, culling words and images that link China's food to California's wine, a child's drawing of a grape to Caravaggio's Bacchus, Colette's gourmandise to an African-American's shortenin' bread. In such a world, we've found unlikely pearls, like a trio of Renaissance ladies embedded in the flesh of America's low-fat kitchen. We hope that the harvest of words and images in this first volume of *Wine, Food & the Arts* furthers the goal of The AIWF, "to reach an ever-increasing audience among those who love good food and good wine." As we look toward the new century, we hope that this new series will provide an annual harvest home in which we celebrate the many ways that the arts of good wine and good food nourish our minds and hearts — as well as our bodies — and link our daily pleasures to the timelessness of art. ⌒

BETTY FUSSELL

The thing that sets Robert Mondavi apart is the force of his will. *Driven forward by his fierce spirit, he has done three lifetimes' work in one: establishing a world-class vineyard; creating the most important Anglo-French link in the wine business; and supporting the well-being of his industry with unmatched generosity, working tirelessly to nurture — in the somewhat stony soil of late 20th-century America — the belief that wine is a pleasurable, civilized, healthy drink. He is to cabernet sauvignon what Admiral Rickover was to the nuclear submarine, what Henry Ford was to the family sedan.* **There is also a second defining characteristic.** *Bob Mondavi is a super-salesman, no doubt about that, and full of the energy and the palaver of the breed. But he also has the passionate conviction that many salesmen lack, the belief that his product has all the virtues he attributes to it. Sure, he was born into the wine trade, but he stayed in it, despite adversity, because he loves his product. Watch him sip a really fine glass; watch his eyes sparkle; listen to him describe the vine to his companions. It has to be love, because only love can sustain such exuberance for decades.*

R.W. APPLE JR.

THE BLOOM OF A TASTE BUD

Seen by scanning electron microscope, our taste buds look as huge as volcanoes on Mars, while those of a shark are beautiful mounds of pastel-colored tissue paper — until we remember what they're used for. In reality, taste buds are exceedingly small. Adults have about 10,000, grouped by theme, (salt, sour, sweet, bitter), at various sites in the mouth. Inside each one, about 50 taste cells busily relay information to a neuron, which will alert the brain. Not much tasting happens in the center of the tongue, but there are also incidental taste buds on the palate, pharynx and tonsils, which cling like bats to the damp, slimy limestone walls of a cave. Rabbits have 17,000 taste buds, parrots only about 400, cows 25,000. What are they tasting? Maybe a cow needs that many to enjoy a relentless diet of grass. **At** the tip of the tongue, we taste sweet things; bitter things at the back; sour things at the sides; and salty things spread over the surface, but mainly up front. The tongue is like a kingdom divided into principalities according to sensory talent. It would be as if all those who could see lived to the east, those who could hear lived to the west, those who could taste lived to the south, and those who could touch lived to the north. A flavor traveling through this kingdom is not recognized in the same way in any two places. If we lick an ice cream cone, a lollipop or a cake-batter-covered finger, we touch the food with the tip of the tongue, where the taste buds for sweetness are, and it gives us an extra jolt of pleasure. A cube of sugar under the tongue won't taste as sweet as one placed on the tongue. Our threshold for bitter is lowest. Because the taste buds for bitter lie at the back of the tongue; as a final defense against danger they can make us gag to keep a substance from sliding down the throat. Some people do, in fact, gag when they take quinine, or

Distinguishing between bitter and sweet substances is so essential to our lives that it has burst through our language – children, joy ...a lover ...are "sweet."

drink coffee for the first time, or try olives. Our taste buds can detect sweetness in something even if only one part in 200 is sweet. Butterflies and blowflies, which have most of their taste organs on their front feet, need only step in a sweet solution to taste it. Dogs, horses and many other

animals have a sweet tooth, as we do. We can detect saltiness in one part in 400, sourness in one part in 130,000, but bitterness in as little as one part in 2,000,000. Nor is it necessary for us to recognize poisonous things as tasting different from one another; they just taste bitter. Distinguishing between bitter and sweet substances is so essential to our lives that it has burst through our language – children, joy, a trusted friend, a lover all are referred to as "sweet." Regret, an enemy, pain, disappointment, a nasty argument all are referred to as "bitter." The "bitter pill" we metaphorically dread is likely to be poison.

Taste buds got their name from the 19th-century German scientists Georg Meissner and Rudolf Wagner, who discovered mounds made up of taste cells that overlap like petals. Taste buds wear out every week to ten days and we replace them, although not as frequently over the age of 45 – our palates really do become jaded as we get older. It takes a more intense taste to produce the same level of sensation, and children have the keenest sense of taste. A baby's mouth has many more taste buds than an adult's, with some even dotting the cheeks. Children adore sweets partly because the tips of their tongue, more sensitive to sugar, haven't yet been blunted by years of gourmandizing or trying to eat hot soup before it cools. A person born without a tongue, or who has had his tongue cut out, still can taste. Brillat-Savarin tells of a Frenchman in Algeria who was punished for an attempted prison escape by having "the forepart of his tongue ...cut off clear to the ligament." Swallowing was difficult and tiring for him, although he could still taste fairly well, "but very sour or bitter things caused him unbearable pain."

Just as we can smell something only when it begins to evaporate, we can taste something only when it begins to dissolve, and we cannot do that without saliva. Every taste we can imagine – from mangoes to hundred-year-old eggs – comes from a combination of the four primary tastes plus one or two others. And yet we can distinguish between tastes with finesse, as wine-, tea-, cheese- and other professional tasters do. The Greeks and Romans, who were sophisticated about fish, could tell just by tasting one what waters it came from. As precise as our sense of taste is, illusions can still surprise us. For example, MSG doesn't taste saltier than table salt, but it really contains much more sodium. One of its ingredients, glutamate, blocks our ability to taste it as salty. A neurologist at the Albert Einstein College of Medicine once tested the amount of MSG in a bowl of wonton soup in a Chinese restaurant in Manhattan, and he found 7.5 grams of MSG, as much sodium as one should limit oneself to in an entire day.

After brushing our teeth in the morning, orange juice tastes bitter. Why? Because our taste buds have membranes that contain fat-like phospholipids, and toothpaste contains a detergent that breaks down fat and grease. So the toothpaste first assaults the membranes with its detergent, leaving them raw; then chemicals in the toothpaste, such as formaldehyde, chalk and saccharin, cause a sour taste when they mix with the citric and ascorbic acids of orange juice. Chewing the leaves of the asclepiad (a relative of the milkweed) makes one's ability to taste sweetness vanish. Sugar would taste bland and gritty. When Africans chew a berry they call "miraculous fruit," it becomes impossible to taste anything sour: Lemons taste sweet, sour wine tastes sweet, rhubarb tastes sweet. Anything offputtingly sour suddenly becomes delicious. A weak enough solution of salt tastes sweet to us, and some people salt melons to enhance the sweet flavor. Lead and beryllium salts can taste treacherously sweet, even though they're poisonous and we ought to be tasting them as bitter.

No two of us taste the same plum. Heredity allows some people to eat asparagus and pee fragrantly afterward (as Proust describes in *Remembrance of Things Past*), or eat artichokes and then taste any drink, even water, as sweet. Some people are more sensitive to bitter tastes than others and find saccharin appalling, while others guzzle diet sodas. Salt cravers have saltier saliva. Their mouths are accustomed to a higher sodium level, and foods must be saltier before they register as salty. Of course, everyone's saliva is different and distinctive, flavored by diet, whether or not they smoke, heredity, perhaps even mood.

How strange that we acquire tastes as we grow. Babies don't like olives, mustard, hot pepper, beer, fruits that make one pucker or coffee. After all, coffee is bitter, a flavor from the forbidden and dangerous realm. To eat a pickle, one risks one's common sense, overrides the body's warning with sheer reason. *Calm down, it's not dangerous,* the brain says, it's novel and interesting, a change, an exhilaration.

Smell contributes grandly to taste. Without smell, wine would still dizzy and lull us, but much of its captivation would be gone. We often smell something before we taste it, and that's enough to make us salivate. Smell and taste share a common airshaft, like residents in a high rise who know which is curry, lasagna or Cajun night for their neighbors. When something lingers in the mouth, we can smell it, and

Regret… is referred to as "bitter."

when we inhale a bitter substance – a nasal decongestant, for example – we often taste it as a brassiness at the back of the throat. Smell hits us faster: It takes 25,000 times more molecules of cherry pie to taste it than to smell it. A head cold, by inhibiting smell, smothers taste.

We normally chew about a hundred times a minute. But, if we let something linger in our mouth, feel its texture, smell its bouquet, roll it around on the tongue, then chew it slowly so that we can hear its echoes, what we're really doing is savoring it, using several senses in a gustatory free-for-all. A food's flavor includes its texture, smell, temperature, color and painfulness (as in spices), among many other features. Creatures of sound, we like some foods to titillate our hearing more than others. There's a gratifying crunch to a carrot stick, a seductive sizzle to a broiling steak, a rumbling frenzy to soup coming to a boil, an arousing bunching and snapping to a bowl of breakfast cereal. "Food engineers," wizards of subtle persuasion, create products to assault as many of our senses as possible.

Committees put a lot of thought into the design of fast foods. As David Bodanis points out with such good humor in *The Secret House,* potato chips are: "an example of total destruction foods. The wild attack on the plastic wrap, the slashing and tearing you have to go through is exactly what the manufacturers wish. For the thing about crisp foods is that they're louder than non-crisp ones …. Destructo-packaging sets a favorable mood …. Crisp

The mouth is …the door to the body, the place where we greet the world, the parlor of great risk.

foods have to be loud in the upper register. They have to produce a high-frequency shattering; foods which generate low-frequency rumblings are crunchy, or slurpy but not crisp…."

Companies design potato chips to be too large to fit into the mouth, because in order to hear the high-frequency crackling you need to keep your mouth open. Chips are 80 percent air, and each time we bite one we break open the air-packed

cells of the chip, making that noise we call "crispy." Bodanis asks: "How to get sufficiently rigid cell walls to twang at these squeaking harmonics? Starch them. The starch granules in potatoes are identical to the starch in stiff shirt collars …whitewash …is …near identical in chemical composition …. All chips are soaked in fat …. So it's a shrapnel of flying starch and fat that produces the conical air-pressure wave when our determined chip-muncher finally gets to finish her chomp."

These are high-tech potato chips, of course. The original potato chip was invented in 1853 by George Crum, a chef at Moon Lake Lodge in Saratoga Springs, New York, who became so angry when a guest demanded thinner and thinner French fries that he sliced them laughably thin (he thought) and fried them until they were varnish-brown. The guest loved them, envious fellow guests requested them, word spread, and ultimately Crum started up his own restaurant, which specialized in potato chips.

The mouth is what keeps the prison of our bodies sealed up tight. Nothing enters for help or harm without passing through the mouth, which is why it was such an early development in evolution. Every slug, insect and higher animal has a mouth. Even one-celled animals like paramecia have mouths, and the mouth appears immediately in human embryos. The mouth is more than just the beginning of the long pipeline to the anus: It's the door to the body, the place where we greet the world, the parlor of great risk. We use our mouths for other things — language, if we're human; drilling tree bark if we're a woodpecker; sucking blood if we're a mosquito — but the mouth mainly holds the tongue, a thick mucous slab of muscle, wearing minute cleats as if it were an athlete. ❧

Dante Gabriel Rossetti, Prosperine   2

Dante Gabriel Rossetti, Day Dream   7

REINHART WOLF

WOLF

Photo

Journey from

China

An artist who will always be remembered for his anthropological work with food, Reinhart Wolf was one of Europe's leading photographers. In China he documented the vast variety, the exotic culture and tradition of the country's food, and the art involved in creating ancient Chinese cuisine. OPPOSITE: A young pig, China's primary meat, on its way to Guilin's free market. PAGES 10/11: Preserved in lime, salt, ash, seasoning, soda and tea, and stored in a clay pot, these eggs will be edible for six months. PAGE 12: Rice harvester carries bundles home for drying in Guilin. PAGE 13: Village woman with a basket of Chinese horse chestnuts in Kunming.

Colette and Wine

ALICE WOOLEDGE SALMON

"I was very well brought up. As first proof of such a statement, I'll tell you I was no more than three when my father offered me a glassful of the sunburnt wine from his native Midi: le muscat de Frontignan. Illumination, capsizing of the senses, revelation for the taste buds! This baptism made me wine's worthy convert. A little later, I learned to drain my tumbler of mulled wine, perfumed with lemon and cinnamon, while dining off boiled chestnuts. Hardly able to read, I spelled out each drop of aging and graceful bordeaux rouges and dazzling Yquem; then came the murmuring froth of champagne, springing in pearls of air across birthday and first communion banquets to celebrate the grey truffles of la Puisaye .... A good education, from which I progressed to judicious familiarity with wine, never gulped and swilled, but measured into slim glasses and absorbed by sips at reflective intervals." **Colette** presents her credentials, and this is clearly no imposter: We recognize that vital memory, the seasoned judgement, her sinewy prose that culls and offers bouquets of the senses, that leisured perception.

When Colette died — 30 years ago as I write — she was hugely famous, a French glory equal to the Arc de Triomphe, cherished by her readers and dear to folk for whom the name meant little more than animals, butterflies and the plot of *Gigi*.

In these 30 years, certain countries have discovered Gastronomy, their women been Freed from Fetters, their citizens swopped their All for Pleasure and Colette has found a new and often facile public, for whom a fair amount of nonsense has been written about her marriages, numerous liaisons and multiple careers, her supposedly melting sensuality and gastronomic self-indulgence.

Colette was *gourmande,* emotionally attached to large loaves of crusty bread and hand-pressed butter...

She was certainly unique, her personality lacking in banality to a degree most people would find hard to tolerate — "You can't imagine what it's like to live with a woman who is always barefoot," said her second husband — and the most casual reading of three or four of her fifty-odd books and sheaves of essays proclaims that Colette was *gourmande,* emotionally attached to large loaves of crusty bread and

hand-pressed butter, lacquer-red cherries, honeyed figs and the slow-cooking dishes of rural Burgundy, their secrets whispered among housewives at vinous country weddings and rarely recorded. She loved cheese, water chestnuts and a bewitching old *daube* from Provence, which simmered beef, bacon and garlic with "oil that lurks in the sauce and wine which gives it splendor, a special fragrance."

But Colette was a paradox, a mistress of living whose material was not nature, but the world as she felt and transformed it by a highly polished — a dramatic — subjectivity. In his review of Robert Phelps's *Letters from Colette,* Peter Quennell speaks of remembering William Hazlitt's tribute to Falstaff, "a character …whose 'body is like a good estate to his mind, from which he receives rents and revenues of profit and pleasure.'" This was exactly Colette, as much as the austerity and sense of measure that lined her enjoyments, the rigor of her judgments — "I don't like what is easy" — the love of work well done and the fear of time, of decay, the ravages of passion. But as years passed, Colette searched increasingly for the correspondence among apparent contradictions, the links between discrepancies of appearance and "reality," and this gives her writing an emotional and even geological complexity — words, phrases, concepts repeated, reinterpreted, shaken out and reassembled, until, as a participant, you realize her work has a degree of structural cohesion that allies it to Proust and Balzac, whose volumes she read and re-read with absorption.

So Colette's thoughts on wine have depths that are not only vinous. The Burgundian enologist, Pierre Poupon, judges her "our most perceptive wine writer," steeped in the qualities of a great taster — the acutely developed eye, nose and palate, the *"memoire affective"* that gathers and composes impressions: "Her works should be the bedside books of professional and amateur tasters, to their much greater benefit than all those pages that preach the mechanics of tasting and never divulge the spirit."

In 1951, Poupon was a member of the jury awarding the *prix littéraire* at the Paulée de Meursault, one of several feasts that celebrate the Burgundy vintage, and that year Colette was chosen for the excellence of her Burgundian writings and the particular essay *Ma Bourgogne pauvre,* which moves from childhood wines to harvests on the Côte d'Or. Together with *Vins* and *En Bourgogne,* published in 1932, *Ma Bourgogne pauvre* forms the heart of Colette's work on this subject.

In two of these essays Colette evokes Sido, her mother and inspiration, who taught her "divination of the hidden treasure" throughout the physical world by fullest employment of the five senses, of which the "noblest, most lucid and uncompromising" became to Colette the sense of smell. Folded away in the 1870s and 1880s at Saint-Sauveur-en-Puisaye, a market town near Auxerre in the Basse-Bourgogne, "bereft of vines" save for some light-hearted vin de Treigny whose stock did not survive phylloxera, the child shot up nimble and receptive, her intuition schooled to the significance of *"le monde matériel, sphérique, bondé de saveurs."*

It was Sido who contributed some *grands crus,* vintage pre-phylloxera, to that "good education." As antidote to the possibility of adolescent pallors, Colette was given unusual tonics: Out of the dry sand of her granite cave, Sido lifted bottles she had hidden from invading Germans at the time of the Franco-Prussian War – "Château-Larose, Château-Laffitte [sic], Chambertin and Corton," of which glass after glass escorted Colette's afternoon *casse-croûte* of cutlet or cold chicken as Sido watched her cheeks flame with the "vinous glories of France."

Sido was Colette's source, the fountainhead of her life, the recipient of her constant letters until Sido's death before the Great War, and the parent to whom in middle age Colette began to return through the writing of such books as *La maison de Claudine, La naissance du jour* and *Sido.* As a child at night in the garden, Colette had watched her mother beside a drawing-room lamp and realized that "this hand and this flame and the bowed and troubled head …are the center and secret from which grow and spread …the warm *salon,* its flora of cut branches and fauna of silent animals; the house … the garden, the village …. Beyond, all is danger and solitude …. Everything is still before my eyes …beneath my fingers." She continues and writes elsewhere of two revered springs, secret and almost invisible in the Puisaye woods: "Even to speak of them makes me hope that at the end my mouth will fill with their savor and that I'll take with me this imagined draught …."

Springs, rivers, water and wine flow in company through Colette's writing: A cellarman, racking the contents of casks, listens for the "sound of a spring," and during the torridly hot *vendange* of Beaujolais, 1947, *la source,* "revered and invisible, faithful, [is] the last refreshment, this year, for panting mountain and exhausted valley." At her Provençal home in the 20s and 30s, "at any hour of the summer, we treated wine like water: 'I'm thirsty, pour me a glass of wine,'" though in *Vins* she

"I'm thirsty, pour me a glass of wine."

writes that "water is for thirst" and wine, a "'…vital tonic, a luxury, the honor of a meal.' Isn't wine itself a nourishment?" Always the tension of contrast and synthesis.

While a sustenance, wine remains a "mystery" that gives clues to the soil's "true flavor," its taste of flint or chalk or that of a sauvignon graft from Bordeaux that sugars and lightens Algerian wine of quite another character. Colette writes, "A vine slip, carried across mountains and seas, fights to keep its individuality and sometimes triumphs over strong mineral elements," and you think immediately of her wrench, aged 20, from Burgundian town to married Parisian bohemian, crushed between the paws of the awful Willy. Deceived, disillusioned and exploited by this fat satyr with such a terror of the blank page that virtually his entire literary output was the work of others, Colette survived in the prison of her marriage, afraid of her husband while continuing, in a way, to love him and learning to endure and to write.

She emerged sound, if battered, from this "jail," Willy's "school," with "the certainty of my flexibility, as I always called my self-control, reckoning that no human resistance can last without the power to give way." When Willy, after 13 years of unhappy alliance, finally told her to go, with "such moderation, so little noise," Colette found herself dazed and expulsed. She waited – fearful – for the call to return that never came and "got used …to thinking that I'd reached the point where the whole flavor of my life must change, as a wine changes its bouquet according to the slope which bears the stock."

Apart from the mysteries of hillside and graft, Colette marveled at the enigma of a Provençal vine-plant caught like a snake between rocks and seemingly nourished by nothing more than dew and sun, and observed Côte d'Or vineyards "stripped bare, in their strict alignment, their fine and disciplined framework" during one late winter, a spring so stealthy that the uninitiated would imagine the vines still slept. "Who would have said that exuberance brooded?" She had, she writes, no thought for an imminent "explosion," pleased that the richest hills of Burgundy, "austere and shrunken" at this turn of season, should so closely resemble the undulating nudity of her own *Bourgogne pauvre* at la Puisaye.

This is Colette with both hands full. Things are not what they seem: "What are appearances, Madame, what are appearances?" says the weird Monsieur Daste, secret ornithocide at the hotel Bella-Vista, whose lesbian proprietors are really man and woman – a rhetorical question that springs the catch on an abundance of ordinary or marginal people, the bourgeois bohemia that crowds Colette's work. "Great men," she writes, are missing; her preference has gone to "the obscure, individuals filled with a sap that they reserved and withheld from banal invitations." These "sapid" characters roused her almost passionate curiosity: A shabby groom, formerly a jockey and down on his luck, looking now like "an old glove," enthralled her with his knowledge of "everything relating to horses and dogs, illnesses, treatments, fiery drinks that would cure or kill, and I liked his substantial conversation, even if he taught me far too much about the way animals are 'painted up' to fetch higher prices."

At an opium den Colette meets Charlotte, a middle-aged courtesan of Renoiresque attributes who feigns public physical abandon to please a young lover, but whose tranquil self-control and kind, bourgeois practicality are her special fascination: "Such clarity of order in what can only be called debauchery would have dismayed another listener." Colette has little trouble with inconsistency; a seamstress who formerly "toured in operetta" – a euphemism for much else – has been reduced to hasty choices and "among all transgressions preferred the unprofitable indulgence of sewing and ironing. The pungence of an employment generally considered innocent can be more desirable than many sins committed through necessity." Colette and the self she dramatized heard the confessions of scores of such people, "so many sources dancing with the truth, tossed about on a rich and unfiltered must."

Colette could be unbearably coy, could affect to believe that "human solicitude" had no influence on a great year among *millésimes* – "there everything is heavenly witchcraft, planetary movement, sunspots." She knew all about such deceptive appearances, that the wintery vineyards of the Côte d'Or teemed with purpose: "Man's hand and thought warm these precious lands, which bear witness to years of human solicitude." Nature is present, but almost always in translation – through the art of Colette's syntheses, the skill of artisans, the artifice of make-up and array. A handsome woman of 45 learns to dress well, apply amber powder and brighten her lips; en route she acquires a first lover. Colette scolds her young daughter for painting her face, and slyly, the child lifts a cluster of grapes, "black through their blue haze of impalpable bloom." These too are powdered, she answers.

Everywhere in the Côte d'Or cellars near the stripped-down vineyards, men are at work, racking and fining the wine, scouring casks by means of heavy chain. Colette describes their industry in some detail, approving the trained instincts and expert gestures: "Only constant and repetitive practice through long years can so refine the human senses." The fruits of so much care profit from time to grow velvety, ardent and succulent, "filled with perfection and memory," and in such writing Colette demonstrates what her third husband called *"son goût pour le travail bien fait."* Her "obscure individuals" – the groom, courtesan and seamstress – are workers of integrity, however bizarre, linked by "a sort of lower-class distinction." Learning to live without happiness, which Colette achieved while married to Willy, "and yet not waste away, is a real occupation, almost a profession." Damien is a Don Juan, his coffers packed with letters from women, his manner reserved and sententious as he demonstrates, for Colette's benefit, the science of seduction; without wit or gaiety, he wears only his "function" and his discreet hatred of the "enemy," woman, with whom he never treats for peace. Colette admires the rigor of his "equilibrium." A pearl-stringer from her native province, Mademoiselle Devoidy, engages Colette's respect for her probity and mocking humor, "the details and surprises of a craft that required two years' apprenticeship, a high degree of manual dexterity and a certain contempt for jewels."

But Colette's interest in work is never far from the value she gives to unrushed time and proportion. Slowness, leisure and idleness are constantly woven through effort – in the Côte d'Or cave, where years are essential to ripen wine, cellarmen move quietly, with "this supreme luxury: …unhurried, reflective rhythm." Gastronomy, she says, is all about savoring; a palate like hers deserves "time to reflect, the leisure to dawdle." Much of her writing unfolds at thoughtful pace – *Chambre d'hôtel, Lune de pluie,* most of *Le blé en herbe, La naissance du jour, Le fanal bleu,* the works about Sido. A woman intrigued by incipient mystery briefly lacks "the leisure" for further indulgence of "extravagant fancies," and a womanizer is assessed succinctly: "Nothing seems shame-

ful, nor even cynical, to eyes of a man — secure in the certainty of a faithful love – who is perfectly at leisure to suffer for a second one."

Here is another of Colette's sweeping themes — love, sex and their intimate partners, decline and self-denial. Janet Flanner's introduction to the English edition of *Le pur et l'impur* speaks of "Colette's desire to add to the limited treasury of truthful insights into love," and often you feel as you read that "she's got it." She was deeply ambivalent about love's necessity and perils. Sido, with memories of a brutal first marriage and a generally scornful attitude toward the male sex – "I like forfeits, such as a wedding, to be surrounded by flowers, music and well-dressed women! It helps to sugar the pill" – had fostered this, and Colette's years with Willy convinced her that delight is penetrated with torment: "So I was

amply punished and soon." Throughout her books love is seen as a "battle" that fascinates; "pleasure" is a "fatal weapon" that "menaces," "throws [one] to the ground" in dread and longing. Men and women fight a "duel," an adoring mistress "suffers" her lover's possession like "torture," a woman about to take a

"I'd reached the point where the whole flavor of my life must change, as a wine changes its bouquet according to the slope that bears the stock."

lover lifts her face to be powdered: "She submitted patiently, sighing as if I were dressing a wound," men are a *"gibier de choix"* – choice game.

Vins pursues this ambivalence – "It's there that as an adolescent I met a fiery, imperious prince, treacherous as all great seducers: le Jurançon" – and *Ma Bourgogne pauvre* carries the metaphor further: At Dijon, during a "glowing September," Colette fell in love at first sight with the city in its plenty and with "Monseigneur le Vin de Bourgogne" strutting through tastevin, glass and goblet. "For three days he never left my side, chose me as his victim – his very willing victim." There are frisson and mystery: A

"In the very wine I drank I looked for you, and never found a Pommery like yours."

"glorious" wine, tasted once in a dark inn, is like the traveler's memory of a night-time kiss, stolen from an unseen stranger.

Among Colette's books, *Le blé en herbe* and *Chéri* – each in its way about love's beginning – move through a sort of sleight of looking-glass to *La fin de Chéri* and *La naissance du jour*, where love is relinquished. *Le blé* is filled with dream and nightmare, the salt air of Britanny and suddenly! the dark, cave-like rooms – shot with resinous scent, red and black and the chill of diamonds – where the adolescent Phil is seduced by a beautifully "virile" Madame

Dalleray. Phil is almost literally abducted, confused by the shock and climate of passion "where whirled an indistinct tumult of colors, perfumes, lights whose hidden source shed a piercing ray or a pale space of discretion." In the grasp of his affair, Phil is intoxicated – "he's eaten opium!" – by "emotions that are lightly called physical," by silk and velvet, a voice, all the *"enivrant superflu,"* from which he drags himself awake, "conscious like a sated drinker who feels, as he moves, the inert sway of wine that has lost its quick and flickering spirit." Three hours strike, falling from the clock like grapes from the bunch, and Phil suffers, enjoys suffering, all the nuances in aftermath of bittersweet sexual pleasure.

Chéri is one of the most artificial of Colette's books, a belle époque conservatory devoted to the "bustling life of idle people," and in my view her most moving achievement. All about the discovery and loss of love between Léa, a stylish courtesan approaching 50, and Chéri, the dandified boy she's "kept" for six years, the pages are suffused with absence and disbelief in the pain of waiting. Age causes frightening damage and *Chéri* ends with the sandy taste of defeat, but throughout there is much tart and buoyant humor, racy dialogue and the resilient, foreshortened writing of Colette at her best. Léa is a woman fond of "order, good linen, wine that has mellowed and well-considered cooking," and for me, all the story's rueful elegance is here: "…he breathed in, remembering, as he opened his nostrils, the rose-perfumed sparkle of an old champagne of 1889 that Léa kept for him alone" and here: "In the very wine I drank I looked for you, and never found a Pommery like yours."

If *La fin de Chéri* is a somber, almost pitiful work, in which the same character, post-World War and "majestic in his decline," strips himself of life to plunge into the source, "the hidden treasure" of Léa's past excellence, long-lost to both of them, it almost parodies *La naissance du jour*, published two years later. *La naissance* is not so much a novel as an experiment in which the middle-aged Colette projects her dramatized self towards an order of fulfillment through renunciation; the whole is based on the *vendange* as a metaphor for the culmination and reflective aftermath of love, gathered up and put aside to slumber in memory like "the cloistered new wine." Age ceases to menace: Colette's hands, rough as a day-laborer's, do not dismay like Léa's, flabby and lined with the network of cracks left on soil by a drought, and men as lovers – the writer's "native country" –

join, or so she hopes, with Sido and the world of plants and animals in a sort of distant and mystic correspondence. "I spent myself [*je me versais*] unstintingly .... This is, I assure you, a very beautiful time in my life ...the grapes are almost ripe ... I must be patient ... — *soignons les crus de mes souvenirs.*" This is a book that strives hard, but in straining toward its total integration achieves an air of contrivance that is absent from the hothouse warmth of *Chéri.*

Appropriately, Colette lived her last Parisian decades in the rue de Beaujolais. Three of her windows, on the second floor of the graceful Palais-Royal, overlooked the semiprivate world of its gardens, and her final handful of years, when she was crippled with arthritis and never out of pain, were cheered by the proximity of the Grand Véfour, a restaurant returned to quality in the late 1940s by Raymond Oliver. Colette and her husband made it their "local," where the lunch she preferred was salmon coulibiac with champagne.

A final word from Colette? "A difficult page, the conclusion of a novel are advantageously served by an exceptionally well-filled glass."

Unknown, Colette dans son Jardin à St. Sauveur-En-Puisaye 14

Unknown, Colette Willy 21

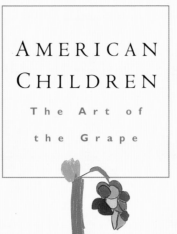

AMERICAN CHILDREN

The Art of the Grape

This art of the grape exhibit celebrates the work of children age five and up. OPPOSITE: **Conner Leech,** Crazy Grape; ABOVE: **Lily Guy,** Grapes on the Vine

James Burke, Green Grapes on a Plate

Sophie Anna Greenberg, Oh! …Splash

Connor Leech, Grapes in Hawaii

Elisabeth Wilkie, Checkered Grapes

The Heartbreak Grape

In which the pinot noir makes its appearance as the heartbreak grape, and some thought is given to where it came from and where it's going.

MARQ DE VILLIERS

When it comes right down to it, all winemaking is similar — it's the process of helping grapes ferment themselves into wine. But, clearly, some methods of encouraging this process are better than others. And some grapes make the job easier than others. The pinot noir is one of the more difficult ones. In those innocent days when gender descriptives were still thought amusing, the pinot noir was called "feminine" — by which was meant flighty, changeable, beguiling and seductive. **In** the same vein, they called it the heartbreak grape because it was so stubborn, so particular, so elusive, so damn difficult to get right. And also because when it was at its best it made the most sublime wine of all. The heartbreak grape? You cannot break a heart without having captured it first. The greatest wines of Burgundy — which is where the greatest pinot noirs have traditionally been elevated — are tantalizing, elusive, poetic, thrilling. Even the most inspired red bordeaux, that cunning mixture of cabernet and merlot, can't fill the head with spiced dreams quite like the great burgundies. No other red wine can balance spice and fruit so …flirtatiously, can seem at once so ripe and fragile, so decadent and clean, so irresistible. And, it's fair to say, no other red wines can drive the poor writer to such extravagant prolixity, as you can plainly see from the foregoing, or from this overblown passage from Oz Clarke:

"The flavors of the great red Burgundies are sensuous, often erotic, above rational discourse and beyond the powers of measured criticism as they flout the conventions in favor of something rooted in emotions and passions too powerful to be taught, too ancient to be meddled with."

To the wine drinker, pinot noirs are robust, vigorous and explosive. But to the winemaker, they are fragile, prone to spoilage, delicate.

Whew!

The heartbreak comes from dim memories of this greatness as producers all over the world, from the valleys of California or New Zealand to the hearty plains of Australia or Argentina, contemplate the thin, mean and insipid wines they have managed to concoct out of the blessed pinot noir. If truth be told, many of the most insipid come only a few meters from the great domaines of Burgundy itself, from lesser slopes or lesser soil or lesser growers and producers taking lesser care.

And equal heartbreak from contemplation of attempts in California to make wines approximating the Big Red One, heavy, stultifying wines tasting of burned plum or, in the words of the British wine writer Jancis Robinson, wines that "smelled unnervingly of burned cabbage."

The capricious nature of pinot noir in the bottle reflects a similar flightiness in the vine itself. Pinot noir mutates if you give it a cross look, seemingly out of pure spite. It's a master of the genetic dance. It's also very old, and no one can any longer say which is the "original" clone; there was pinot noir already planted in the Burgundy area when the Romans pushed gingerly into the deep interior of Gaul – Pliny describes it, in an early bout of critical purple. And Burgundy is now thick with clones of all qualities, after many attempts to fight off the viruses and fungi to which the variety is so prone, blast it.

Some "burgundies" are made with what probably isn't pinot noir at all, but *pinot droit,* an upright clone similar to many invented in California by the techies of Davis, which bears more fruit than the traditional *pinot fin.* There are supposed to be 365 clones of pinot noir now growing along the tight little ridge of Burgundy. Well, that's a neat number – others say there are 200 or 1,000. And, considering that each clone would affect the wine differently because of its particular genetic structure, it's easy to see why this is "a minx of a vine," an exasperating variety for growers, winemakers and critics, as well as the humble wine drinker.

This welter of wines, this passel of pinots, makes standard-bearing and standard-keeping a thankless task. It's further complicated by the pinot noir vine's tendency to degenerate and to die early, sometimes decades before it should. And complicated yet again by pinot noir's notorious reluctance to travel to new climes, where its "feminine" allure seems to pine away into old-maidish rectitude.

That, at least, was the thought a decade or so ago. The problem was, winemakers in these new climes got it all wrong. They plunked the vine down into the arid heat of the California plains, where the poor thing became sunburned and petulant. As a consequence, the early American pinot noirs had size and weight but lacked subtlety, finesse or much character.

If that wasn't enough, the pinot noir is also an early budder with sluggish secondary growth, so spring frosts are deadly. Some years the vines stubbornly refuse to set fruit, the flowers simply withering instead of turning to precious grapes. No one seems to know why.

The pinot noir grape is as capricious as the vine. Its petulance comes from its thin skin. It needs regular sun to ripen, but will quickly overripen if the sun gets too hot. On the other hand, it can't cope with too much rain. It will swell and burst and rot if it gets too wet at harvest time. It's also an early ripener: The longer the grapes can stay on the vine, the more complex the resulting wines, but the tendency to rot in the rain and to burn in the sun greatly elevates the risk. And if it gets too ripe it will lose its fruit flavors and potential for grandeur.

They plunked the vine down into the arid heat of the California plains, where the poor thing became sunburned and petulant.

Color, flavors and tannins are precariously balanced in the pinot noir. Sometimes, the vine seems naturally to produce grapes rich in tannins and anthocyanins, with a deep ruby color. More often, it will produce an insipid rosé the color of antique brick. Climate can effect this swing. So can weather, soil, elevation, sunshine, moisture, pruning, picking, fermentation, filtering and a dozen other things, apparently up to and including the phases of the moon and the moods of the winemaker.

To the wine drinker, pinot noirs are robust, vigorous and explosive. But to the winemaker, they are fragile, prone to spoilage, delicate. The making of pinot noir requires – demands – a deftness of touch that was generally thought to be alien to the California character. Got an A+ in enological studies? The pinot noir won't care. As Steve Doerner once put it: "Since pinot noir starts out as a delicate wine without a strong backbone, every time you do something to it, you strip more of the body out of it. So, if you're striving for a rich, complex wine, the less you handle it the closer you'll come."

With pinot noir, structure is easy to get. It is subtleness, perfume and richness that are the difficult things. Because of this …elusiveness …the making of pinot noir becomes an overriding passion and obsession. Its nature remains a mystery, and it remains the wine that most serious winemakers want to make – and most serious winemakers want to drink.

And there's one other problem with it. It changes, the fickle thing, even in the bottle. Josh Jensen, when he's holding a tasting for important clients, likes to open a bottle the night before to see how it's "performing." This is not a matter of variation between bottles of the same batch, which plagues all winemakers, but that pinot noir is always restless, constantly undergoing changes.

So while everyone recognizes a great pinot noir when they come across one, pinot noir has no single universally accepted flavor or style. In can be pitiful to watch wine writers struggling for acceptable comparatives.

Without trying you can find pinot noir variously tasting of fresh wild strawberries (or, more often, raspberries), of damsons or other plums, of black cherries, of vanilla and butter and violets on the delicate side, of pepper and allspice and truffles on the robust side, and of "earthiness," sometimes off-puttingly described as "farmyard" or "barnyard" or game, or even rotten vegetables. One eminent writer, despairingly, wrote that it "smelled like shit," and meant it, approvingly. Of course, presumably he meant the sweeter odor of the cow and he was likely thinking of hay in a summer barn, but I still think he should have tried again.

Joseph Ward, writing in *Condé Nast Traveler* in September 1992, said of pinot noir that it was "quicksilver to cabernet's iron," a nice phrase. Joel Fleishman, wine *amateur* and Duke University's vice president, wrote in *Vanity Fair* in August 1991: "At their best, pinot noirs are the most romantic of wines, with so voluptuous a perfume, so sweet an edge, and so powerful a punch that, like falling in love, they make the blood run hot and the soul wax embarrassingly poetic." (Well, at least he admitted it.)

The great California winemaker André Tchelistcheff, who can be forgiven the solecism because of his old-fashioned European courtliness,

"At their best, pinot noirs are the most romantic of wines, with so voluptuous a perfume, so sweet an edge, and so powerful a punch that, like falling in love, they make the blood run hot and the soul wax embarrassingly poetic."

once called pinot noir "the wonderful aroma of the inside of a kid glove worn by a young woman." This will not do much for its marketing among female drinkers, but unreconstructed romantic males can see what he means.

Could pinot noir be made to work in California? Tchelistcheff, always good for a quote, once said he'd made a "superb pinot noir [at Beaulieu in Napa], but I don't know how I did it and I was never able to do it again."

Most California pinot noirs are still hot and simplistic, one-dimensional wines; when you hear a California winemaker defend himself by saying he's trying for "a California style," you can be sure he means he was unable to duplicate what he knew in his heart was the real thing. Still, this defensiveness is forgivable. For years Californians smarted from the condescension of the lofty Burgundians. That the French, secure in their centuries-old Gallic superiority, were able to be snottily polite only made it worse – the French have always been able to say "yes, but …" better than anyone. Typical was the haughty Lalou Leroy, co-proprietor of the mighty Domaine de la Romanée-Conti, who, when confronted with a superb pinot noir from Chalone, sniffed, *"Oui, mais c'est chaud."* She later deigned to be "impressed" by Oregon and remembered an Eyrie Vineyards pinot noir that was *"intéressant," "mais assez léger."*

Well, this is all gone now. Madame may sniff, but the more foresighted Burgundians are sending their sons to America and Australia to learn the new ways of doing things. Just as the Californians and the Oregonians learned a hard-won lesson, go back to Burgundy to learn how it's done.

And so, having done precisely that, Josh Jensen (of the Calera Wine Company) joined with Acacia (Chalone), Zaca Mesa, Sanford, Belvedere, Iron Horse and Chateau Bouchaine in Pinot Noir America, a producers' association. They began to make wines as rich and as satisfying as the best of the Old World, wines that smelled of cherries and ripe plums, of chocolate and leather, with the same beguiling sweet silk of the greatest red burgundies, those of the Domaine de la Romanée-Conti or those of Henri Jayer in Vosne-Romanee and Nuits St-Georges. ⌒

Carole P. Meredith, Pinot Noir Grapes   26

Luca Forte, Still Life   31

ANNE SEXTON

Oysters

Oysters we ate,

sweet blue babies,

twelve eyes looked up at me,

running with lemon and Tabasco.

I was afraid to eat this father-food

and Father laughed

and drank down his martini,

clear as tears.

It was a soft medicine

that came from the sea into my mouth,

moist and plump.

I swallowed.

It went down like a large pudding.

Then I ate one o'clock and two o'clock.

Then I laughed and then we laughed

and let me take note —

there was a death,

the death of childhood

there at the Union Oyster House

for I was fifteen

and eating oysters

and the child was defeated.

The woman won.

OPPOSITE: **Henri Matisse,** Tulips and Oysters on a Black Background

IN THE LOW-FAT KITCHEN

JEFFREY STEINGARTEN

Last night I played the neatest trick on my wife. I grilled a slice of my very best home-baked bread, spread it thick with Promise Ultra Fat Free Nonfat Margarine, set it on the counter, sat back and watched. The toasty aroma drew my wife into the kitchen and the sight of a huge slice of rustic bread slathered with a golden spread caused her to smile broadly and pop it into her mouth. I'll never forget the way her smile first froze, transformed into doubt and then into horror as she gagged, stumbled over to the kitchen sink and gave up her delectable rustic bread covered with Promise Ultra Fat Free Nonfat Margarine. What fun we have together!

I learned about Promise Ultra Fat Free Nonfat Margarine, which is made from water, vegetable mono- and diglycerides, gelatin, salt, rice starch and lactose, plus a bouquet of chemicals and artificial flavors, from *Butter Busters* (Warner Books), an extremely popular low-fat cookbook. I have been living with low-fat cookbooks for the past month or so, not because it makes any medical sense, as I will explain, but because the low-fat cookbook business has become a bloated and distended juggernaut that threatens to crush everything else on the market. Susan Arnold of Waldenbooks kindly sent me a printout of their best-selling cookbooks and there, proudly occupying first and second place, were *In the Kitchen with Rosie* (Knopf) and *Butter Busters*. Rosie's book reached its 32nd printing in 8 months, bringing its grand total to 5.8 million copies in print and making it not only 1994's number-one bestseller in all book categories but also the fastest-selling book since Gutenberg. *Butter Busters*, with well over a million copies in print, has nothing to be shy about either. And Susan Powter's completely incoherent

ing suffers in taste and texture. *Butter Busters,* America's second most popular cookbook, gives up more than a bit of taste and texture. It gives up real food itself.

Pam Mycoskie, who wrote and published the book all by herself in 1992 and then sold it to Warner Books in 1994, leaves nothing to chance. Forty pages are taken up by a shopping guide. Pam's picks include Butter Buds, Egg Beaters, Egg Mates, Better'N Eggs, Pillsbury Lovin' Lites cake mixes and frostings, Old El Paso Fat-Free Refried Beans (doesn't "refried" mean anything anymore?), ENER-G egg replacer, Texas B-B-Q seasoned chicken strips, Peter Eckrich Deli "Lite" roast beef slices and non-fat cheeses from Alpine Lace, Borden, Kraft, Polly-O and Healthy Choice. There must be a law against calling them cheese. Have you ever tasted this stuff?

With these and other ingredients you can make Sloppy Joe Casserole, Mashed Potato Shell Taco Pie and Pam's Sweet Trash. Her Pineapple Salad Surprise contains ketchup, fat-free Miracle Whip, lobster tails and Cointreau. I baked Pam's Rich Fudge Brownies because the more opulent Easy Fudge Brownies on the facing page begins with a box of Lovin' Lites Fudge Brownie Mix, which I deemed a form of cheating. As it was, the Rich Fudge Brownies include Sweet 'n Low, Sweet 'n Low brown sugar substitute, Egg Beaters, our old friend Promise Ultra Fat Free Nonfat Margarine and Braum's Lite Fudge Topping. In the end, the brownies turned out sticky and rubbery and would have had no chocolate taste without the Lite Fudge Topping. Even mediocre brownies

Why does the world need a flood of painfully self-righteous and badly written cookbooks to teach us how to avoid three pats of butter a day?

Food (Simon and Schuster) soared onto the bestseller list immediately upon publication.

Most – probably all – low-fat cookbooks contain long self-congratulatory passages claiming that the author's revolutionary new way of cooking actually tastes better than real food. This is only rarely true. Sure, many traditional dishes should have been lightened years ago. But most of today's low-fat cook-

have a brief half-life in my house; five days on, the pan of Pam Mycoskie's Rich Fudge Brownies sits lonely on the kitchen table.

Why would Americans want to humiliate, degrade and befoul themselves by eating these dishes or any of the hundreds of fat-free packaged foods that Pam recommends to her million readers? Why did a million of us buy her book?

Because we have become mortally afraid that eating fat will make us fat, bring on heart attacks, give us cancer. Fearful equally of death and unsightly bulges, we are no longer able to distinguish right from wrong. In the ignorant grip of a national fat phobia, we recoil from the flesh of the velvet green avocado, the benign and perfumed olive and the golden oil of the crunchy peanut as though these were the moral equivalent of the thick carpet of solid white fat surrounding a slab of beef. "A low-fat lifestyle is as important to you as stopping smoking," Pam opines. This is dangerous nonsense.

What are the facts?

Heart disease is not linked to the total amount of fat you eat. It is associated only with saturated fat, the kind derived from animals and perhaps from some tropical plants, like the coconut and the palm. This has been known for 40 years.

The heart-disease rates of various countries are not linked to their total fat intake. In the famous Seven Countries study, the island of Crete showed the lowest rate of heart disease in the world, even though its diet was very high in fat — most of it from olive oil. Today the countries with the lowest rate of heart disease are Japan and France. Japan historically has had a very low-fat diet, France a high-fat diet.

National rates of heart disease are most closely linked to consumption of dairy fat and meat.

Not all fat classified as "saturated" will raise your cholesterol level. Cocoa butter, the main fat in chocolate, only slightly increases your bad LDL cholesterol. God's in his heaven; all's right with the world.

A low-fat diet can be dangerous for patients with adult-onset diabetes. A study published in May, 1994, in *The Journal of the American Medical Association* showed that, contrary to the low-fat, high-carbohydrate diet then recommended by the American Diabetes Association, diabetics can lower their level of blood sugar, triglycerides, insulin and LDL cholesterol on a diet very high (45 percent of calories) in monounsaturated fats — olive oil, canola oil and so on.

As much as 25 percent of the population is "insulin resistant," which means that they gain weight more readily from eating carbohydrates than from eating fats.

Consuming lots of omega-3 fatty acids (the oil in marine fish and some plants, like purslane) has been shown in some (not all) studies to greatly reduce your risk of coronary disease. But low-fat diets restrict you to lean fish that lack omega-3.

Countries with a low-fat intake do show lower cancer rates, but the link is with animal fat and meat consumption rather than with total fat or vegetable fat.

National rates of breast cancer increase with a higher consumption of total calories, not fat intake. In a recent Greek study, women who consumed olive oil more than once a day had a 25 percent lower incidence of breast cancer than women who consumed none.

Colon cancer rates are associated in some studies with animal-fat consumption, in other studies with red meat; there is no link with vegetable fat. Similar results have been found with prostate cancer.

Obesity does not seem to be related to fat intake. In a comparison of 65 counties in China, no link was found between the fat intake of a particular population and its tendency to become overweight — even though some groups consumed less than 5 percent of their calories in fat. Southern European countries show both lower fat consumption than northern European countries and higher rates of obesity.

In a recent clinical trial at the University of Minnesota involving moderately obese women, a low-fat diet showed no significant advantage over a low-calorie diet. Some studies claim an initial advantage to a low-fat diet, but the difference typically disappears after a few weeks. Research at Rockefeller University has found no difference in the amount of weight experiment subjects gain or lose on liquid diets that are high or low in fat.

...not to force every single dish into a low-fat straitjacket

In the ignorant grip of a national fat phobia, we recoil from the flesh of a velvet green avocado, the benign and perfumed olive, and the golden oil of the crunchy peanut...

To summarize: Saturated fat is bad for your health; red meat and dairy fat are the worst; unsaturated fats are perfectly OK; olive oil is probably beneficial; your body weight is unlikely to be affected by the percentage of total calories you consume in the form of fat.

If all this is true, then how did the mass frenzy of anti-fat paranoia begin? What keeps it going?

There is enough blame to go around. The National Research Council's authoritative and influential 1989 report, *Diet and Health,* correctly targeted saturated fat in some chapters but grossly misrepresented the medical literature in others, warning, without foundation, against total fat consumption above 30 percent of calories. The argument is often heard that if we warn the public to lower its total fat consumption, it will automatically lower its saturated-fat intake. This simply compounds

Obesity does not seem to be related to fat intake.

everybody's misconceptions about diet, making it much harder to eat happily and well. The new FDA food labels are just as bad, putting total fat on lines one and two, leaving saturated fat until line three.

And then there are cult figures like Dr. Dean Ornish and Susan Powter. Dean Ornish made his mark in the late 1980s by demonstrating, over the skepticism of many in the medical profession, that a program of smoking cessation, moderate exercise, stress reduction (including meditation), social support and a very low-fat diet could reverse the progress of arteriosclerosis and lessen the risk of coronary heart disease, without surgery or drugs. His credentials as a diet doctor are much less impressive. Ornish's very lucrative *Eat More, Weigh Less* (HarperCollins) is a low-fat, vegetarian cookbook preceded by 81 pages full of misleading information. Since in his earlier research with heart patients he never bothered to isolate the relative benefits of diet, exercise, smoking cessation and so forth, Ornish's own work is irrelevant to the draconian diet (10 percent fat) he prescribes. Instead, his footnotes abound with references to newspaper accounts of other people's research.

Ornish's Life Choice program "takes a new approach, one scientifically based on the type of food rather than the amount of food." This is, of course, the same "new" approach about which every one of the hundreds of low-fat cookbooks that clog the market boasts. The difference is in the fanaticism of the Ornish diet: You must avoid meats of all kinds (including fish), all oils (saturated, monounsaturated and polyunsaturated — it doesn't matter to Ornish), avocados, olives, nuts and seeds, even low-fat dairy, alcohol and other products with more than two grams of fat per serving. "No matter what you may have heard," he writes, "olive oil is not good for you." I remember attending a nutrition conference with Ornish in Boston a few years ago. An expert panel was struggling with the serious and difficult question of whether olive oil really confers benefits that other vegetable oils do not. As though he had been unwilling or unable to absorb the complexities of the argument, Ornish could contribute nothing other than claiming that olive oil must be harmful because it is a fat. He seems to be fixated and obsessed.

Dean Ornish's disregard of the medical literature has not diminished his influence. One casualty is Sarah Schlesinger and her *500 Fat-Free Recipes* (Villard Books) which was a solid seller. Referring to Ornish and more vaguely to studies from "societies around the world," Schlesinger has become irrationally convinced that cancer and heart disease (plus acne, rashes, vertigo and "hormonal imbalance") automatically spring from consuming "excess" fat. She offers us this urgent advice so we can follow her diet even on trips abroad: "Learn the necessary phrases to express your needs. For instance, you can say 'All my food must be fat-free' around the world in one of the following languages:

> Spanish: Es necessario que mi comida no tenga grasa.
> German: Mein Essen darf kein Fett enthalten.
> French: Tout doit être preparé sans gras.
> Italian: Niente douvebbe essere fritto"

Ms. Schlesinger needs a new advisor in the Italian language.

Contrary to Ornish and his polyglot epigones, there is not much to be gained from cooking the low-fat way, so the corresponding pain had better be extremely minor. Absence of pain is the chief criterion I used while cooking for a month from low-fat cookbooks. I chose *In the Kitchen with Rosie* and *Butter Busters* because they have sold more copies than any other cookbooks in recent memory. The pain suffered in using — even reading — *Butter Busters* was so excruciating that no gain, perhaps not even immortality, would make it worth cooking from.

What do these authors mean by low-fat cooking? The American Heart Association and the 1988 Surgeon General's Report both call for us to get no more than 30 percent of our calories from fat. This seems a good cutoff, and most low-fat cookbooks aim for it. But, as the average American takes in about 37 percent of his or her calories from fat, cutting down to 30 percent does not seem like a drastic step. It works out to just over a tablespoon of olive oil, or three pats of butter. Why does the world need a flood of painfully self-righteous and badly written cookbooks to teach us how to avoid three pats of butter a day? If you insist upon a low-fat diet, your objective should be to average out your consumption to 30 percent or whatever your fat goal is, not to force every single dish into a low-fat straitjacket. But that is how most low-fat cookbooks take a very modest goal and make it very difficult to attain.

Grease is good. Grease works. As all low-fat cooks discover, fat serves a remarkable number of purposes: It blends and softens flavors, carries them about the mouth and allows them to linger; in cooking, it conducts heat more effectively than water and allows temperatures high enough for the delicious browning reaction to occur; and it contributes to texture in obvious and less obvious ways.

In a recent clinical trial …a low-fat diet showed no significant advantage over a low-calorie diet.

Without fat, some flavors become oddly aggressive. In desserts, sugar tastes sweeter, but eliminating sugar makes for drier textures — because sugar retains water. Fat holds and stabilizes flavors — low-fat desserts can become tasteless after brief storage, and any inferior ingredients in them will be exposed.

It takes a very good cook to eliminate fat.

Jonathan Koch, Ultra Low-fat Cook   34

Jacopo Palma Vecchio, The Three Sisters   38-39

ADRIENNE
RICH

Peeling

Onions

Only to have a grief
equal to all these tears!

There's not a sob in my chest.
Dry-hearted as Peer Gynt
I pare away, no hero,
merely a cook.

Crying was labor, once
when I'd good cause.
Walking, I felt my eyes like wounds
raw in my head,
so postal-clerks, I thought, must stare.
A dog's look, a cat's, burnt to my brain —
yet all that stayed
stuffed in my lungs like smog.

These old tears in the chopping bowl.

OPPOSITE: **William H. Johnson,** Still Life with Onions, Jug, and Fruit

INNARD BEAUTY

R. W. APPLE JR.

Sydney Smith, the 19th-century English cleric, once defined heaven as "eating …foie gras to the sound of trumpets." For me, you could hold the trumpets. Much as I adore caviar and white truffles, foie gras is the extravagance I crave most. Not, you health cops, because it's the most fattening of the three. I love it best because it's my madeleine. Along with Romanesque cathedrals, foie gras was my first big discovery when I went to France as a kid. I never take a single silken bite without thinking back to the early 1950s, when I thought all liver came from calves and all cathedrals were Gothic. Foie gras makes me feel young again, in other words. And it makes me feel, in the immortal words of Bob Strauss, the Texas politician, like "a rich sumbitch." **People** have been nuts about foie gras — it's pronounced "fwah grah" and means "fat liver"— since antiquity. Egyptian paintings from 2500 B.C. show farmers holding geese by the neck and force-feeding them balls of grain. The Romans gave their geese figs to obtain what they called *tecur ficatum,* or liver with figs, and the modern Italian word for liver, *fegato,* derives from the Latin word for fig, not liver. According to several sources, the Romans brought flocks of geese from Picardy in northeastern France to their capital, herding them across the Alps on foot. Waverley Root ridiculed that tale as something out of Mother Goose – or to be more precise, out of Alexandre Dumas, whom he dismissed as "a slipshod writer" who had misread Pliny the Elder.

To make foie gras today, selected birds – Toulouse or Strasbourg geese or moulard ducks, which are a cross between Muscovys and Pekins – are kept in a confined space at a constant temperature and fed grain through a funnel jammed down their gullets. The geese develop livers weighing up to 2½ pounds, instead of a few ounces, and the ducks yield

On a sweltering day last August, Faison complained that the birds were going through a rough patch. "They have the audacity to sweat…"

livers of a pound and a half or so. This drives the animal-rights people to distraction, or at least to hyperbole. Last year, an official of People for the Ethical Treatment of Animals, based in Rockville, Maryland, was quoted in the *Washington Post* as saying, "Every country has its brand of cruelty. In England, it's fox

hunting. Italy is veal central. And in France, they stuff geese full of grain until they explode."

The best foie gras used to be pretty much confined to France; the American lover of the stuff had either to travel there (or to a nearby country) or be satisfied with something in cans or jars. Today we are more fortunate. Though the bacteriophobic United States still forbids the importation of foreign foie gras in raw form, superb duck foie gras is produced in upstate New York. Goose foie gras, more difficult and twice as costly to make, is not yet produced here on a commercial basis.

Foie gras is turned out in Israel, Canada, Poland and Hungary – even Madagascar – in addition to France and the U.S. But it is in France, and especially in Alsace, and in Périgord and Gascony, that something of a cult has grown up around it. Winter is the peak season for goose production, and that is when you find the birds and livers proudly laid out in the weekly markets in southwestern towns like Eauze and Périgueux. Consumption soars at the same time; eating foie gras has become a traditional holiday treat, a centerpiece of the French celebrations on Christmas Eve and New Year's Eve.

Goose liver *(foie gras d'oie)*, more traditional than the duck variety and more opulently rich, is preferred by many chefs if they plan to serve it cold. But duck foie gras *(foie gras de canard)* holds its texture and flavor better when cooked, and now accounts for 80 percent of the global output. Jean-Louis Palladin, who used to cook at a Michelin two-star restaurant in Condom, in the heart of foie gras country, and who now runs the much-lauded Jean-Louis at the Watergate Hotel in Washington, D.C., says that the difference between the stuff he used in the old country and what he buys here is "minimal." He serves 40 pounds of New York State foie gras a week in a restaurant seating 42 people.

Chef André Daguin, of the Hôtel de France in Auch, is considered the high priest of foie gras in the French southwest – so it seems fitting that his daughter Ariane has put American foie gras on the map. Her firm, D'Artagnan, Inc., of Jersey City – founded a decade ago in a disused meat-packing plant – doesn't raise its own ducks, but distributes livers produced by Hudson Valley Foie Gras in the Catskill Mountains, an hour north of New York City. Last year, D'Artagnan sold $16.5 million worth of foie gras and other duck-based products and, says Daguin's partner, George Faison, they have barely scratched the surface. The business is not problem free, however. On a sweltering day last August, Faison complained that the birds were going through a rough patch. "They sweat," he said. "They have the audacity to sweat, and they lose fat instead of turning it into bigger livers!"

When the great Fernand Point prepared foie gras at his La Pyramide in Vienne in the old days, he simply marinated it for 24 hours in port, armagnac, salt, pepper and nutmeg, put some truffles in the center, wrapped it in a thin cloth coated with chicken fat and poached it gently in a *bain-marie.* No one else's foie gras has ever tasted quite as good as Point's – except maybe that served at Au Trou Gascon in the 12th arrondissement of Paris, or at L'Ami Louis, a dingy bistro in a melancholy corner of the 3rd arrondissement. At L'Ami Louis, there are three slabs per order – three sturdy slabs of firm, cool, pink liver, edged with golden fat that tastes as good as the thing itself, served with rough slices of baguette grilled over a wood-burning fire. They ask only a week's pay for it.

When it is sautéed – becoming crisp on the outside and puddinglike on the inside – foie gras is transformed. And in this form, it seems to go with almost anything, as long as there is some acidity or salinity involved to cut its inherent richness – coarse salt, capers, salsify, plums, arugula.

Wolfgang Puck combines foie gras with pineapple and cinnamon at Chinois on Main in Santa Monica; Jean Georges Vongerichten teams it with mangoes at Vong in New York City. But I once ate a horrid preparation of foie gras at, of all places, André Daguin's Hôtel de France: foie gras with blackberries. The gritty seeds of the fruit spoiled the liver's texture, which is a lot of what foie gras is about. DiMaggio sometimes struck out, and so, that time, did Daguin.

The lily can be gilded; Michel Guérard, the brilliantly inventive chef who runs a leafy pleasure dome at Eugénie-les-Bains in the wooded area south of Bordeaux known as the Landes, used to make a pot-au-feu of vegetables and foie gras, in which the liver partially melts into the bouillon. (Larry Forgione, who once worked for Guérard, does an American interpretation of the dish at his An American Place in New York City.) Marc Meneau at Vézelay in Burgundy, another three-star practitioner of the chef's art, serves sinful little deep-fried beignets, crisp on the out-

side with liquefied foie gras in the center. Not to be outdone, Marie-Claude Gracia, a fifth-generation chef who runs a rustic little inn called La Belle Gasconne in the village of Poudenas (*pop.* 274), makes the mother of all pasta sauces: slices of foie gras and morels in a reduction of crème fraîche, ladled over tagliatelle.

When it is sautéed… foie gras is transformed.

Unhealthy, you say? Cholesterol city? Not according to a ten-year study by the French National Institute of Health and Medical Research, completed in 1991, which found that southwestern France – where they eat lots of fat livers, and drink lots of red wine and armagnac (and smoke like chimneys) – had the country's lowest death rate from cardiovascular disease.

But even the French don't argue that foie gras is the most easily digestible thing in the world. Don't eat too much of the stuff, my advice is, and certainly don't eat it too late at night. On the other hand, it is said that Bismarck used to drink a glass of milk and eat a slice of foie gras to cure his insomnia. No wonder they called him the Iron Chancellor. ∼

Unknown, Painting from the tomb of Nebamun 44

ELIZABETH RICE

British Botanicals

Elizabeth Rice is an award-winning British botanical illustrator renowned for her elaborate and precise watercolor studies. Honored by the Royal Academy of Botanical Illustration, her artwork has been featured in *Crops of Britain and Europe,* among other works. OPPOSITE: **Elizabeth Rice,** Apples and Pears

ABOVE: **Elizabeth Rice,** Onions and Other Vegetables (detail)

Elizabeth Rice, Potato, Aubergine and Winter Cherry

Elizabeth Rice, Onions and Other Vegetables

THE GLEANERS

That first season the gleaners came out only at sundown. They parked their vehicles, battered Chevrolets and rusted Datsun pickups, well away from each other on the road that ran by the field. Caps pulled low on their foreheads, gunnysack shawls across their backs, the gleaners crossed the ditch and entered the field. Under a pink and blue sky, the air belled with September chill, the gleaners had eyes only for the ground, for the black, heaved furrows, the damp and tangled vines at their feet. They had come to look for potatoes that the mechanical harvester had missed or discarded. **There** – a fat, muddy russet, big as a man's hand. There – in the trough of the irrigator's wheel, another fat one. There – in a clump of vines, two smaller potatoes. Ahead – beside a heavy stone brightly scarred, among a small maze of boot-prints and a blacker stain of oil, a whole scattering of potatoes. **Stoop,** stoop, and stoop again: In this way the gleaners moved down the field. Their progress was measured against the dark silhouette of the irrigator, its long drooping lengths of pipes and tall stilt legs. Intermittently, like prairie dogs rising for a quick look, the gleaners stood fully erect to measure their distance from the other pickers and from the road and their own cars. Then they quickly bent again to their work. In the fading light, humps grew on the gleaners' backs as the weight of potatoes stooped their shapes ever lower until, in the purple dark, they staggered back to their cars. Sacks thudded. Trunk lids slammed. Engines raced and gravel chattered sharply against wheel wells as their vehicles accelerated away without headlights toward the highway.

The second season the gleaners came out earlier in the evening. Some appeared already in the afternoon, and the boldest waited in their cars beside the potato fields as harvesters worked the last rows. Word was that Universal Potato Company didn't care. It had bigger things to worry about, things like hot spots in

In the fading light, humps grew on the gleaners' backs as the weight of potatoes stooped their shapes...

one of the storage bins, nailing down the Burger King contract, the union sniffing around. Universal Potato wasn't about to bother people who picked up a few stray spuds. Just don't drive in the fields or otherwise pack down

the dirt — that was the unofficial word. Otherwise, have at them. Plenty of spuds for the taking. Enough for the whole town of Flatwater (population 2,650) — that was the word in the cafés and stores on Main Street. With spuds free for the picking, why would a person even fool with potatoes at home in the garden?

That second autumn other types of vehicles began to drive slowly along the potato fields. These were newer, shinier cars: Ford sedans, late-model Pontiacs, an occasional older Cadillac. Often they stopped, amber parking lights on, radios playing faintly through open windows as the cars' occupants watched the gleaners. The spectators were mostly older retired couples, people like Shirley Anderson and her husband, John.

"Look at them," Shirley remarked, staring past her husband at the gleaners. "Don't it remind you of the depression?" She was seventy-four, had short white curly hair, and wore a gauzy blue head scarf set loosely over her permanent and knotted tightly at the chin. She was neatly dressed in knit pants, blouse, and sweater. Out of the side of her eyes she watched for her husband's reaction.

John's heavy white eyebrows dropped slightly as he squinted. He remained silent, hands wrapped around the steering wheel.

"You wouldn't think, in modern times like these, a person would ever see this, would you?" Shirley said, clucking her tongue briefly. She watched as a heavyset woman stooped for a potato, then another and another like a fat old hen picking her way across a chicken yard. She plucked six spuds in quick succession. Shirley felt her heart pick up a beat.

"Depression days are coming again," John said. He clenched the steering wheel and his fingers reddened. "Things can't go on the way they are!"

"Some people would agree with you," Shirley said quickly. She didn't want to anger him, have him drive off. It had been difficult enough getting him to take her on the dirt roads past the potato fields. Their car was a white 1976 Oldsmobile with 24,532 miles on the odometer and no rust spots or paint chips — a town car. Shirley did not drive. She had never had a license.

"I mean, why can't people raise their own food, like we do?" She turned the angle of her vision an inch so as to watch him more closely. He continued to stare out into the field somewhere. Shirley turned her eyes back to the gleaners. The fat woman dragged her gunnysack forward. Shirley's heart beat slightly faster still, and she reached underneath her sweater to touch the plastic bag that she had brought along.

"Easier to steal them, everybody steals nowadays," John said. His voice rose sharply.

Shirley swung her gaze away, out her side window and across the road to a drifting hawk that she pretended had caught her interest. With John she had to go carefully. At age seventy-nine he was an increasingly silent, unpredictable man. Conversation with him was like speaking with their son who lived in Alaska. His phone was hooked up to a satellite, and the words had to bounce off something (was it the earth or was it the satellite? she could never remember), then float back. There was a delay. You had to wait. You couldn't talk fast and you couldn't interrupt.

"Though," Shirley said evenly, looking back to the potato field, "you couldn't really call it stealing, could you?" She paused. "I mean, Universal would just plow them under, wouldn't they?"

John stared across the field. Shirley watched the fat woman shake a clump of potato vines. Dirt showered in the sunlight.

"Their potatoes are poison," John said. "The chemicals!"

Shirley waited. She watched the big woman stoop five more times, then drag her bag forward, leaning into the task, using both hands now.

"Oh, I don't know about that," Shirley said, drawing in a little whistle of air through her teeth to show that she wasn't in a hurry or in any way serious about the topic at hand. "Some people say they taste just as good as homegrown." Inside her sweater, she gathered up the plastic bag.

A car came toward them from behind. Shirley turned quickly to look at the battered pickup that rattled past, its dust rolling briefly upward, then tilting slowly toward the ditch. John, staring into the sunset, did not even turn his head.

She eyed her husband for a long moment, then said, "Maybe we should give them a try." She laughed briefly — loud enough so that he was certain to hear. "Why don't I just step out there and find us a couple spuds for our supper?"

In the silence a small airplane droned overhead. Its single red light blinked slowly across the sky, crawling toward the Dakotas. Suddenly John's hand dropped from the wheel onto the gearshift and the car lurched forward.

They passed a second potato field where a shiny blue car parked in the shallow

Sacks thudded. Trunk lids slammed.

ditch drew Shirley's eyes. A car from town. A familiar car, though she couldn't put the person's name to it. The owner, a well-dressed woman about her own age, with white hair and pink scarf tied at the chin, was a few yards behind in the field. She carried a white plastic grocery bag that could only come from Marketplace Food and Deli, the new grocery store in town. Shirley leaned forward through her window to squint at the woman who, at the same moment, looked toward the road. It was Thelma Haynes, a widow who worked in the floral shop at Marketplace Food and Deli. Their eyes locked. Thelma turned quickly away toward the field; Shirley ducked her head out of sight below the car's window.

John turned to stare at her. Shirley pretended to see something on the floor, then sat up straight again. The car moved on. As they drove she kept her eyes peeled, as usual, for cars over the center, for farm implements or stray animals on the road, but her mind was filled with another vision: Thelma Haynes's plastic grocery bag. It was blooming white on top, hanging dark and heavy below. Slowly Shirley's gaze swung around to the interior of the Oldsmobile. She began to stare at the steering wheel. The dashboard. The levers. She watched the pedals. How he positioned his feet. She knew which pedal stopped the car, which gave it gas. The brake. The gas pedal. Two pedals, two feet. She looked at the shift lever. The little window above the steering wheel said, "P R D 2 I." Momentarily she thought of the "Wheel of Fortune" game show. How most people chose the letters "R S T L E." How she often figured out the phrase long before the contestants. How most things could be figured out if a person paid attention. She looked back to her husband's hands, where he positioned them on the steering wheel.

Later, as they drove on blacktop, a heavy, deep-fat smell drew her gaze to the Universal Potato Company, a long, airport-hangar-sized building that stood at the edge of town. Its walls were concrete, windowless panels, and high atop the gray front was the company's symbol, a giant potato, which radiated yellow-painted sunbeams from its brown body. Above the potato, steam billowed from vents and shiny turbines that spun out a hot, starchy smell of french fries. It was the odor of progress — the aroma of jobs.

Universal Potato had come to northwestern Minnesota from Idaho where the land was tired and the water expensive. Around Flatwater, the land, graded perfectly flat by some long-ago glacier, was fresh, sandy loam on top with clean gravel below and a water table that rose up to within twenty feet of daylight. The combination was ideal for irrigation and big machinery. It was a wonder, Shirley thought, that farmers around here had not thought of growing potatoes themselves.

But people, especially farmers, were creatures of habit. Before potatoes this land had supported only dairy cows, and barely enough of them for farmers to scratch out a living. Shirley had grown up on such a farm — the white house, the red sheds, the black hills of manure that rose up in winter behind the barn. In spring the manure went back onto the fields and the whole country stank so strongly that, while waiting for the school bus, her eyes had always run tears; if she tied her head scarf across her face to cover her nose, bandit style, then her hair had smelled of manure when she arrived at school. There were kids, rough-looking boys and tomboy girls, who had always smelled of the barn because they did chores before school, and she had steered clear of them. Her friends were town kids.

After high school Shirley took a teller's position at First Farmer's Bank and married John Anderson, who ran the hardware store. Her bank was the most modern building in town with its fluorescent lights and a continual, cool, humming breath of air-conditioning. In town the only time she had to smell manure was when farmers came in for their loans.

Looking back, something Shirley did often after she retired, she saw a trend among the farmers who came to the bank. It had to do with the smell of manure. In the 1950s only a few farmers came in for loans, and they stank strongly of cow dung and occasionally of DDT. In the 1960s more farmers came for loans. They smelled sweeter and dustier with the scent of commercial fertilizers such as nitrogen, phosphate, and sulfur, along with the orange-rind aroma of 2,4-d, the brush and slough-grass killer. In the 1970s, when First Farmer's grew in assets from $1 million to $6 million, the farmers had come in droves. More chairs were added to the waiting room, and their fabric soon gave off the sharper, nose-itching smell of agrichemicals: herbicides; pesticides;

Atrazine, Roundup, Lorsban. By the end of the 1970s the odor of manure was gone altogether. Farmers dressed better, sometimes even wearing ties for their meetings with the loan officers. By 1980, when First Farmer's built its new building and simplified its name to First Bank, the farmers had at long last joined modern times. And Shirley, as retired chief teller, was proud to have played a part.

Of course, with changing times some things were lost. The twenty-cow dairy farm had pretty well disappeared by 1975, and even forty cows were hardly enough nowadays. But an omelet could not be made without first breaking the eggs; survival of the fittest, that was the way Shirley saw it. The farmers who could adapt changed to irrigation. Square fields turned round under the slowly circling irrigators that sprinkled corn day and night through July and August. Dairy barns, empty of cows, their stanchions removed, now leaked number-two yellow corn from their windowsills and ventilators. Farmers read market news, went to seminars in Minneapolis or Fargo, stayed in touch with world events.

Those who didn't lost out, went under. In the bank Shirley had seen it close-up. If it was sad initially – the dispersal auctions in particular – a farmer losing his land wasn't as bad as people had made it out to be, for then the potato growers had arrived. Universal Potato Company gave top prices for irrigable land and usually gave the farmers jobs besides. Farmers stayed on in their own homes, continued to work their own land. Now they drove tractors and harvesters that belonged to Universal Potato, and they no longer had to worry about maintenance, about breakdowns, about the high price of parts. In the evening there were no barn chores, no more getting up at midnight to birth a calf. For the first time in their lives, the men had time to watch TV, to go fishing on occasion or drive their families on a Saturday afternoon over to the mall in Fargo.

In Flatwater the stores improved. A Hardee's came to town, and Marketplace Food and Deli followed. An antique store opened on Main Street where old milk cans and separators were the best sellers. Sometimes Shirley browsed through the store, clucking her tongue at the things people would buy. A pedal grindstone. Blue mason jars. Wooden kraut cutters. Washboards. She wondered what had become of things like her family's old ice chest, the crank phone; some items were worth an astounding amount of money. But antiques were a laugh. Shirley had grown up with antiques.

Why would she want to buy them back? She had no desire to return to the old days. To depression days. To the flat frozen fields, the black winter mountains of manure.

The next morning, early, Shirley woke up with a vision of white. Frost. She sat up in bed, remembering she had not covered the squash or the muskmelons. Quickly she dressed, put on a jacket and rubber boots, and went out. A white rime of frost coated the steps, and beyond it – she saw immediately – the tall squash plants lay flattened and brown in the garden. On their shrunken vines the cantaloupes sat up high and shiny like skulls. She muttered under her breath.

In the wet, flattened garden, the only green was a row of peas and carrots that

But an omelet could not be made without first breaking the eggs; survival of the fittest, that was the way Shirley saw it.

John had planted. Somehow, in planting, he had gotten the seeds into the same trench. In June the row had come up frothy green like a wave of seawater rising from the garden, threatening to spill over everything. By late July the row had crested, collapsed under its own weight, and delivered no peas and no carrots. It remained now in September so dense and junglelike that even frost could not penetrate it.

No matter. The garden was finished now, and good riddance, Shirley thought. She looked briefly back to the house, then around at the neighborhood. The houses nearby were narrow, white and tall with dark, steep-pitched roofs and caragana and lilac bushes rising up untrimmed toward the windows where shades remained pulled; their neighbors, all older couples like themselves, were still sleeping. They weren't worrying about gardens and frost. All of them had long ago figured out that it was cheaper to buy food. John and Shirley had the only garden. Once she had drawn up a list of garden expenses for John. It had sent him into a rage, and she had not spoken of it again.

Now she walked along the mess of pea vines and carrots to the four rows of potatoes where there was a plant here, a plant there.

"You're too old to plant a garden, just like I'm too old to work in one."

Long gaps of weedy dirt between. Had he planted them too deeply? Cut the seed potatoes wrong, left them with no eye? Put the eye staring down, sent its white shoot on a death march to China? It didn't matter now.

Shirley went to get the wheelbarrow for the squash and melons. In the garage she paused by the Oldsmobile. In the dim light

from the window, the car's paint glowed whitely. She ran a finger along its roof, then down the cool window glass to the chrome door handle. Quietly opening the door, she eased into the driver's seat. Her heartbeat immediately picked up speed. She raised her hands to the steering wheel. The little grooves – how well they fit the fingers! She turned the wheel left and right. She sat there staring through the windshield and the garage window, beyond which she could see only sky and the vague, darker peaks of the neighbors' roofs. She sat there until she heard shouting in the garden.

She blinked.

"They're stealing!" John was shouting. Shirley scrambled from the car and found John in the garden in his pajamas, with no jacket, no shoes, shouting.

"The kids, they're stealing again!" He waved his arms.

"Here! Hush!" Shirley called. "Stop that crazy talk!"

"The kids," John said. "Look at the garden. It's all gone."

"There's no stealing because there's nothing to steal," Shirley said. She grabbed his arms, and her words came out faster than she wanted, but she couldn't slow them down or pull them back. "That stealing stuff is all in your mind because your mind is not so good anymore – you can see that by the way things are planted."

John let his eyes fall slowly to the thick green row of peas and carrots. "You're too old to plant a garden, just like I'm too old to work in one," Shirley said. "Things change and you've got to get that into your head. Don't you see," she said, softer now, "we're old. Old."

In a long, slow turning of his head, John brought his gaze around to hers. The morning light shone in his eyes, and for an instant she saw him as he had been when he was a young man. Then he looked down, down to his own hands. He stared at his fingers, his palms, turned them over, then back, then over again.

She went to him. "Come on in," she said.

He let himself be led into the house.

Later in the morning, since it was Saturday, they went grocery shopping as usual. John drove. Shirley watched him warily, but he drove well enough, and they arrived at Marketplace Food and Deli without trouble.

"You want to come in this time?" Shirley said.

John looked across the parking lot to the new store.

Marketplace had slanting copper-colored angles to its metal roof and several colored flags flying on top; it was what Shirley imagined a Spanish train station must look like. There was also a drive-up window for grocery pickup that kept people out of the rain and snow and sun. And under one roof, it offered a bakery, coffee shop, florist's shop, video section and film-processing station, as well as the deli and grocery aisles that went on and on under bright fluorescent lights.

"Too big," John said. "A person could get lost in there."

"Well, sit there then," she said with some relief. "I'll be right back. You got that?"

Halfway across the parking lot, she looked back to see him, alone in the car, nodding yes.

Inside the store, from the smell of the bakery Shirley realized she had not finished her own breakfast. Now she had to shop on an empty stomach, something she tried never to do; it always ran up the grocery bill. She found a cart and, before moving an inch, made herself read aloud the list. "Crisco. Yeast. Baking soda. Flour. Milk. Turkey (leg). Navy beans. Hand soap."

In produce she passed by eggplants, jalapeño peppers, kiwifruit, artichokes, gingerroot, guavas — who in this town ate such things? Briefly she hefted an avocado, then put it back. At home she had jars and jars of perfectly good green beans and tomatoes and pickled carrots. She found Idaho red potatoes, a ten-pound plastic bag for $3.99! She hefted the bag, held it up toward the light. The potatoes were all as firm and round as apples and scrubbed a fresh, chapped red. She thought of the scattering of her own potatoes — droopy, sprouted and brown — that remained in the root cellar. She let the bag of Idaho potatoes balance on the edge of her cart. She turned it sideways for another look. Finally she thudded the sack back onto its shelf.

In fruits she passed baby coconuts, Asian pears, papayas and other odd-duck items until she reached California seedless grapes. Still sixty-nine cents a pound, though down a nickel since last Saturday. She moved on. Blue plums caught her eye, and she stopped to smell them, squeeze their little purple bellies. Her own stomach growled. She swallowed, checked her list, then tore off a plastic bag and chose two of the fattest plums.

The turkey leg took longer. "Most people want the breast," the manager said cheerfully. He was a round-faced man who wore a white plastic hat with a short bill; as he dug through the freezer bin, the round white packages clacked against each other. "I'll have to look in back," he said.

As she waited, she added up the total so far, then thought about eating one of the plums. But it would not be washed, and, besides, someone might think she was not going to pay for it.

The manager appeared in the doorway. "Fresh or frozen?"

"Frozen," Shirley said quickly.

Heading toward hand soap, she passed through the feminine-products section, shelf after shelf of shields, liners, rinses, all packaged with drawings of women in white dresses in a sunny field of daisies or at the seashore where their long hair blew lightly in a breeze. She thought of her own cotton that she washed every month, of it hanging on the far end of the clothesline, waving in the wind during the summer, swinging stiffly in winter. Today there was none of that for her. As she passed by the little plastic boxes and packets, she had to look twice to figure out what some of the things were for.

In the soap section she sneezed twice — had to steady herself against her cart until the dizziness passed. Coming down the final aisle, Shirley was so hungry that she held tightly to the cart and let it pull her along. Rounding the corner, she smelled flowers and at the same moment saw Thelma Haynes. Thelma was dressed in a white apron with a fresh carnation on her blouse, her hair done up far too blue; she stood polishing the glass counter of the floral shop.

"Shirley Anderson," Thelma called out in an artificially cheery voice, "what can I do for you today?"

"Me? Oh, no, just the groceries," Shirley said.

"Special on fresh carnations," Thelma said brightly.

"I grow my own flowers," Shirley said immediately. The fool idea that she didn't drove away her hunger.

"Well, they are cheaper that way," Thelma said, lowering her voice. A young manager-type fellow passed. He wore a short-sleeved white shirt and a thin black tie, and Thelma turned quickly to adjust some dried flowers in a fancy teakettle pot.

"Everything is too high-priced," Shirley said.

Thelma fussed with the stems. Weeds really. Spray-painted weeds.

"Take potatoes," Shirley said, narrowing her eyes slightly. "Nearly forty cents a pound."

For a moment Thelma was silent. Her small blue eyes flickered briefly around her before they came back to Shirley. "I guess it depends on where you get them," Thelma said.

"Yes, I suppose it does," Shirley said.

"You know how many potatoes I've got?" Thelma whispered. Her eyes widened momentarily, a sudden surge of light.

Shirley held tighter to the cart's handle.

"Twelve bushel. Maybe fifteen. They take up the whole closet and part of the bedroom of my apartment," Thelma said. She giggled briefly.

Shirley felt the grocery cart push her backward an inch.

Thelma leaned forward across her counter. "I tell myself I won't go out there again," she whispered, "but the next thing I know, there I am."

"You could give some away!"

Thelma narrowed her eyes.

"Other people, who can't get around by themselves, they might like some of those potatoes," Shirley said. She leaned slightly forward.

Thelma turned sideways to wipe at something on the glass, then gave Shirley a sidelong look. "I don't know. I've got myself to think of."

"Fifteen bushel!" Shirley said.

Thelma blinked and for a moment her eyes widened again as they took in the store behind — the aisles, the displays, the people with their carts, the children. "No one knows what's going to happen," she whispered. "You could live on potatoes if you had to."

At the till Shirley waited behind a heavyset woman with a cart topped off with two twelve-packs of Mountain Dew. She breathed lightly through her mouth as she watched the cashier swing the items across the red light that burned beneath the counter. The beeping went on and on. To speed things up when her turn came, Shirley counted out exact change: $13.68. She clutched the money. Her hand shook slightly. Ahead, as the beeping of the groceries went on, the fat woman stood leafing through a Teen Beat magazine; she had no idea of what things cost, Shirley realized. What kind of person did not know the price of things? She felt a fine cool sweat begin to come on her forehead.

When Shirley at last passed through the electric doors, the grocery boy behind her, the wide parking lot outside tilted for an instant — then righted itself — then tilted again.

"Lady, are you all right?" the boy said. His voice sounded faraway.

"Of course I'm all right," Shirley said. "Just a little hungry."

For some reason he grabbed her, roughly, and the next thing she saw was his face staring down at her. She was lying on the asphalt.

"Call 911!" the boy was shouting.

"No!" Shirley said sharply. The cost of an ambulance gave her a surge of energy, and she sat up. "Those are my groceries," she said quickly to the boy. Her sack lay tipped over on the asphalt. She struggled to her feet and shook her finger at him. "I paid good money for those!"

At twilight, in the chilly, silent yard, Shirley stood beside their bedroom window and listened. She had slept all afternoon, and now it was John who snored on. He was out for the night. And so was she.

Wearing one of his old caps and carrying a flat flour sack over her shoulder, Shirley went to the garage. There she stowed the bag in the trunk of the Oldsmobile, then got behind the wheel. Taking a deep breath, she started the engine.

Its noise made her flinch and duck her head for a moment. Then she looked up, swallowed, and began to back out of the garage. On the street she paused to catch her breath, then put the little arrow on "D" and got ready. She wrapped her fingers tightly around the wheel, her fingernails biting back into her palms, and felt her heart beating around and around the wide, hard hoop of the wheel. Or maybe it was the humming pulse of the engine she felt. Swallowing once more, she took her foot off the brake.

She crossed Main Street without event. On the side streets, each time a car approached she held her breath and, at the last moment as they passed, jammed shut her eyes. Remarkably, when she opened them, the street was clear again.

As she headed toward the city limits, two cars flashed their lights at her. Then a third. Was she too far over? What was she doing wrong? Cars passed her from both directions, sometimes tooting, sometimes flashing their lights. The headlights! She began to pull buttons along the dashboard — the wipers came on — until yellow beams shot down the road in front of her. After that she set her jaw and brought the Cutlass up to forty.

In a few minutes she began to look for the dirt road that was smaller, narrower, farther off, a flat dusky plate with an occasional looming grove of trees, and she almost missed the road. Turning sharply, the car tilted over the corner, bounced once on something — a stone — that clinked underneath, then found the gravel road again. She drove another mile, then another and another. About to turn back, she saw, in silhouette, stretched across the field, the long black spine of an irrigator.

A car was just pulling away from the field. Shirley sped up suddenly, then braked to a halt with a final lurch. From the bottom of her sack she lifted the cool heavy cylinder of the flashlight, checked its beam, then headed quickly down and across the ditch. She had not walked twenty steps before the narrow beam of her light speared a potato.

Then another.

And another.

Rapidly she dropped them into the sack.

But they were so small. In the next moment she realized that these were potatoes other people had passed by. She dumped them from her sack and headed deeper into the field. Ten minutes later she found a furrow that no footprints had followed, and there she began to find real potatoes. Heavy-bodied russets. One would make a

She had not walked twenty steps before the narrow beam of her light speared a potato.

meal. She began to think of them that way. Meal.

Meal.

Meal.

Meal.

She hurried forward, following her light, stooping and stooping again, the sack bouncing on her back. In what seemed no time, the neck of the sack began to chafe sharply across her shoulder, and her arm was cramping.

She stopped. She looked back toward the road where the Oldsmobile, small and far away, drew light from the falling dark and glowed like a lighthouse beacon. She

Other memories, images from childhood, rose up from the darkness.

pressed on. Three more, she told herself — three more good ones. One by one she found them — five, actually — then made herself turn back.

By the time she reached the Oldsmobile, her breath came in short gasps. Her arms were numb. She slumped against the car and tried to breathe evenly. It took her several minutes to regain her strength, and as she stared off across the dark she gradually came to see how few lights there were on the land. A white pinprick of a yard lamp here and there. Four, possibly five farms if she looked in all directions. That was all.

She began to think of neighbors from her childhood. The van den Eykels. The Lanes. The Grunheims. The Niskanens. The Petersons. She wondered what had become of them. Other memories, images from childhood, rose up from the darkness. The bright Surge milking kettle that her father had swung from cow to cow. The oiled leather surcingle strap from which the milker had hung like a second belly beneath the cow. The Watkin's salesman with the glass eye and the sweet jars of orange and purple nectar that her mother had bought from him. The slivers of ice her father had chipped from the blocks that he fished, with black tongs, from beneath wet sawdust. The April melting, the wide field ponds where she and the other farm kids had sailed shingle boats with corn-shuck sails. Where had it all gone?

She had grown up, of course, and things had changed, as they must. Still leaning against the trunk, she looked back toward Flatwater. Her town glowed under a fuzzy cap of orange. Those new sodium-vapor streetlights. The town did not need to be lit up so brightly, she suddenly thought, and certainly not all night. One needed just enough light to see by. She switched on her flashlight again and turned its beam far out into the night. Where its light stopped, she imagined, was where the present ended and the past began. She thought about that for a moment. Abruptly she swung the light back into the trunk. Its yellow glow bobbed in steady rhythm as she began to count potatoes. Afterward, she shouldered the empty sack and turned the light, once again, onto the dark field. ~

Gary Kelley, Hard Scrabble Farmer   52

Gary Kelley, Farmscape   63

PABLO
NERUDA

Ode

to Wine

Day-colored wine,

night-colored wine,

wine with purple feet

or wine with topaz blood,

wine,

starry child

of earth,

wine, smooth

as a golden sword,

soft

as lascivious velvet,

wine, spiral-seashelled

and full of wonder,

amorous,

marine;

never has one goblet contained you,

one song, one man,

you are choral, gregarious,

at the least, you must be shared.

At times

you feed on mortal

memories;

your wave carries us

from tomb to tomb,

stonecutter of icy sepulchers,

and we weep

transitory tears;

your
glorious
spring dress
is different,
blood rises through the shoots,
wind incites the day,
nothing is left
of your immutable soul.
Wine
stirs the spring, happiness
bursts through the earth like a plant,
walls crumble,
and rocky cliffs,
chasms close,
as song is born.
A jug of wine, and thou beside me
in the wilderness,
sang the ancient poet.
Let the wine pitcher
add to the kiss of love its own.

My darling, suddenly
the line of your hip
becomes the brimming curve
of the wine goblet,
your breast is the grape cluster,
your nipples are the grapes,
the gleam of spirits lights your hair,
and your navel is a chaste seal
stamped on the vessel of your belly,
your love an inexhaustible
cascade of wine,
light that illuminates my senses,
the earthly splendor of life.

But you are more than love,
the fiery kiss,
the heart of fire,
more than the wine of life;
you are
the community of man,
translucency,
chorus of discipline,
abundance of flowers.
I like on the table,
when we're speaking,
the light of a bottle
of intelligent wine.
Drink it,
and remember in every
drop of gold,
in every topaz glass,
in every purple ladle,
that autumn labored
to fill the vessel with wine;
and in the ritual of his office,
let the simple man remember
to think of the soil and his duty,
to propagate the canticle of the wine.

PAGE 64: **Vivienne Flesher,** Neruda's Wine Glass

The Welcome Table

JESSICA B. HARRIS

African-Americans have a love affair with food perhaps unequaled in the history of this country. For centuries we've brought the piquant tastes of Africa to the New World. With particular relish we eat, *nyam,* "grease," and "grit," whether it's a bologna sandwich and a peanut patty tucked into the bib of a pair of overalls for a workman's snack or a late-night supper of chitlins and champagne eaten off the finest bone china. Some of us delight in a sip of white lightning from a mason jar in a juke joint, while others delicately lift little fingers and savor minted iced tea or a cool drink while fanning and watching the neighbors on the front porch. Good times or bad, food provides a time for communion and relaxation. **It's** so much a part of our lives that it seems at times as though a Supreme Being created us all from a favorite recipe. There was a heaping cupful of cornmeal to signal our links with the Native Americans, a rounded tablespoon of biscuit dough for southern gentility, a mess of greens and a dozen okra pods for our African roots and a good measure of molasses to recall the tribulations of slavery. A seasoning piece of fatback signals our lasting love for the almighty pig and a smoked turkey wing foretells our healthier future. A handful of hot chilies gives the mixture attitude and sass, while a hearty dose of bourbon mellows it out and a splash of corn liquor gives it kick. There are regional additions, such as a bit of benne from South Carolina, a hint of praline from New Orleans and a drop from at least twelve types of barbecue sauce. A fried porgy, a splash of home-made scuppernog wine and a heaping portion of a secret ingredient called love fill the bowl to overflowing. When well mixed it can be either baked, broiled, roasted, fried, sauteed or barbecued. The result has yielded us in all hues of the rainbow, from lightly toasted to deep well done.

A way with food ...that migrated from the American South to the West in the saddlebags and stew pots and iron skillets of the Buffalo Soldiers and chuckwagon cooks.

With a start like that, it's not surprising, then, that we have our own way with food. We've called it our way for centuries and incorporated our wondrous way with food and eating into our daily lives. We have rocked generations of babies to sleep crooning "Shortenin' Bread," laughed to the comedy of "Pigmeat" Markham and "Butterbeans" and Susie, danced the cakewalk, tapped our feet to the rhythms of "Jelly Roll" Morton, shimmied with wild abandon to gutbucket music in juke joints or sat down with friends and chewed the fat. We've had the blues over the "Kitchen Man," longed to be loved like "Lilac Wine" and celebrated with "A Pigfoot and a Bottle of Beer."

In short, we've created our own culinary universe: one where an ample grandmother presides over a kitchen where the pungent aroma of greens mixes with the molasses perfume of pralines, and the bubbling from a big iron gumbo pot punctuates her soft humming. This is a universe where Aunt Jemima takes off her kerchief and sits down at the table, where Uncle Ben bows his head and blesses the food and Rastus, the Cream of Wheat man, tells tall tales over a "taste" of whiskey. It's the warmth of the kitchen tempered by the formality of the dining room, and the love of a family that extends over generations and across blood-lines. With the improvisational genius that gave the world jazz, we have cooked our way into the hearts, minds and stomachs of a country.

Our way with food is a way with a long history. It is a way that has deep roots extending back over millennia to ancient and almost unknown civilizations, one that found its way through the kitchens of the royal houses of Kush and Meroë, sat down to dine with the Askias of Mali and supped with the princes of Songhai. It is a way with food that at times produced meals so sophisticated that they astonished travelers who recorded them in their accounts. Our culinary odyssey is one of survival and evolution. It took to its hearths the new foods that came from the West and adapted them to its tastes and needs. It survived the privations and sorrows of the Middle Passage and indeed triumphed over them, creating a style of cooking that is immediately recognizable to the taste buds, one that has left an indelible imprint on the cooking of another hemisphere.

It is a way with food that marked the cooking of the plantation Big Houses throughout the United States and, indeed, throughout the hemisphere, one that migrated from the American South to the West in the saddlebags and stew pots and iron skillets of the Buffalo Soldiers and chuckwagon cooks. It rode the burgeoning railroads north and west into the consciousness and palates of the entire country, where many still retain fond memories of meals served by black hands to the accompaniment of rackety-clackety train wheels. In many cases, unbeknownst to the diners, these meals were also prepared by black hands. It marked the tastes of many Americans in the late 19th and early to mid-20th centuries through the foods that housekeepers prepared for charges in homes North and South, and in meals prepared by unheralded family cooks. Finally, in the 60s and 70s it came out of family kitchens to be celebrated as survival food or soul food and derided at the same time as the food of enslavement. The 80s and 90s see our way with food being transformed once again, from daily bread to festive fare, as many people change their diets for health or religious or time concerns. Yet, our way with food endures. It endures because it is a microcosm of our history. It combines the improvisational impulses that gave the world jazz with the culinary techniques of the African continent. It combines the African taste for the piquant with the American leftovers from sorrow's kitchens. It combines the bite of hot sauces with the mellow savor of barbecue, and a sweet tooth with a special touch for baking that has enhanced generations of church tea tables, captured more than one husband and changed untold sylphlike silhouettes into more matronly contours.

This constantly evolving transformation from *tchingombo* (the Umbundu word for okra) to gumbo brings with it all the recollections of a heritage where survival depended on the ability to make the best of a bad lot, where a desire to live higher on the hog kept more than one person going and where generations of African-American cooks both female and male helped us all to survive with their ability to quite literally transform a sow's ear into something wonderful.

It began in Africa, in the area near Al Fayyum in Egypt, where millet was cultivated as far back as 4000 B.C. While the African larder was significantly smaller prior to the Columbian Exchange, there were many indigenous foods: sorghum (a variant of rice), pumpkins, calabashes, gourds, okra, black-eyed peas, a range of leafy greens, melons and watermelon (*Citrullus lanatus*). By the 14th century there were also turnips and cabbages, eggplants and cucumbers, fava beans, chick-peas and lentils, and fruits like tamarind, wild lemons, oranges, dates and figs. There was oil from sesame seeds and the oil palm tree, which also provided palm wine. To spice things up, there were native peppers called "grains of paradise" (*melegueta*), Ashanti and guinea pepper. For an extra buzz, there was kola (*Cola acuminata*) to chew.

After the voyages of Columbus, the larder expanded to include New World foodstuffs such as tomatoes,

...the bite of hot sauces with the mellow savor of barbecue...

corn, chilies, peanuts and yams, all rapidly integrated into the cooking of the African continent. The period of the slave trade was marked by a second exchange of foods. North American slavers commonly fed their slaves rice and corn, both available in Africa and in America, along with black-eyed peas. British ships fed their cargoes horse beans mixed with lard, turned into a pulpy mash and covered with "slabber sauce." William Richardson, in *A Mariner of London,* speaks of his experiences aboard a slaver:

"Our slaves had two meals a day, one in the morning consisting of boiled yams and the other in the afternoon of boiled horse beans and slabber sauce poured over each. This sauce was made of chunks of old Irish beef and rotten salt fish stewed to rags and well seasoned with cayenne pepper."

In the New World, slaves retained the hearth-cooking methods of Africa and the habit of eating stews and thick soups: one-pot meals accompanied by a starch. Thus, South Carolina slaves, when confronted with cracked rice, tomatoes and vegetables, came up with a red rice that is a New World cousin of Senegal's *thiébou dienn.* When asked to mix rice and black-eyed peas, they approximated Senegalese *thiébou niébé* in Carolina's Hoppin' John.

In cooking not just for themselves but for the lavish tables of the Big House, slave cooks transformed in a subtle but real way the tastes of the American South. Africa's taste for highly seasoned food, Africa's method of frying in deep oil, Africa's use of smoked meats and fish as seasonings, of nuts as thickeners, of okra for stews called gumbos — all these, slave cooks imposed on planters in what Eugene D. Genovese, in *Roll*

Jordan Roll: The World the Slaves Made, aptly calls, "the culinary despotism of the slave cabin over the Big House."

After Emancipation, many thousands of African-Americans, looking for a way out of sorrow's kitchen, headed west and took their foodways with them. Certainly Texas barbecue and the 'cueing of Missouri speak of these migrations, as one third of all cowboys were African-American, many of them cooks and guides, who spread their cooking styles around western campfires.

Other migrants Africanized American dishes by means of the railroad. The Pullman Company bragged in 1917 that it was "the largest employer of colored labor in the world," and railway menus (especially in the South) included ham with pineapple fritters, biscuits, baked sweet potatoes and cream of peanut soup. Those who migrated to factories up North, exchanging Delta Blues for Chicago Blues, took their foods with them into the local markets. Leafy greens like collards, kale, mustards and dandelion, pig parts from snouts to feet or tails to innards: All were reminders, as sure as "grits is groceries," of abandoned Southern homes.

My grandparents were among those who followed this trend, migrating from the plantations of Virginia, where my maternal great-grandfather, Samuel Philpot, had served as a house slave up until the age of 30. Stories he told my mother of his enslavement centered around how he had served President Lincoln at a meal.

On my father's side, I, like one out of every three African-Americans, share ancestry with Native Americans. My great-grandmother, Harriet Hornbeak, was a member of the Cherokee Nation. Two of her grandchildren, Johnny and Bill, became cooks and used their earnings to bring their mother and younger brothers north to Brooklyn, New York, from hard times in Napier, Tennessee.

Food has always played an important role in my family life. My childhood is punctuated with vivid memories of Grandma Harris pulling up peanuts in her small garden plot behind the housing projects in Jamaica, Queens. She brought the South north with her and grew not only peanuts but also black-eyed peas, purpley blue-tinged leafy collard greens and bushes that yielded tiny pods of slimy okra (the only food I never had to eat as a child). There was usually a pot of something simmering on the back of the stove in her tiny apartment kitchen, when she wasn't boiling up a batch of laundry or making her own lye soap. She used Bell's

There was usually a pot of something simmering on the back of the stove... when she wasn't boiling up a batch of laundry or making her own lye soap.

poultry seasoning, Calumet baking powder and Indian Head white cornmeal. Grandma Harris wasn't a particularly good cook, though all of her sons (except my father) worked wonders in the kitchen. However, her beaten biscuits, her skillet cornbread and her collard greens were ambrosial.

My maternal grandmother, Grandma Jones, had attended a women's seminary in turn-of-the century Virginia. Even after she'd raised a family of ten children to adulthood and learned to cut corners and pinch pennies, she still had the culinary airs of the descendant of house servants that she was. Her table featured roasts and heaping platters of fried chicken. She saved money, though, by knowing her grocer and bringing home bags of slightly spoiled bananas to transform into crisp fritters, and tiny seckle pears and overripe peaches to pickle as condiments or just "put up." Nothing went to waste; even watermelon rinds reappeared pickled. Every Saturday, she'd prepare industrial quantities of hot rolls. There was always good eating at her house.

At home, my childhood meals were bracketed by my mother's sophisticated tastes (learned at her mother's table and honed as a dietetics student at Pratt Institute) and my father's steadfast refusal to eat anything his momma hadn't cooked in his youth. At parties there were rolled sandwiches with olives and multi-hued cream cheese, silver platters of delicately fluted hors d'oeuvres and grapefruit bristling porcupinelike with skewered orange-cheese morsels, rosy shrimp and tangy anchovies. On weeknights, there might be lamb chops and broccoli or neckbones and white potatoes or, as a special treat for my father, okra.

When African-American cooking came out of the closet in the 60s, I, like most African-Americans, was not surprised at its savory delights. After all, only its name had changed. At my grandmothers' houses, it hadn't been called soul food, it was simply dinner. It was only later — *much* later — that I realized that it was also survival food, the food that took African-Americans from slavery to the present.

And now, in the last decade of the 20th century, there is a new influx of immigrants into the United States. People of African descent arriving from the Caribbean, from Brazil and from the many countries of Africa itself are adding new African-inspired foods to the mix. African-American food has taken on an international outlook: Our meals can be as sophisticated as leg of *lamb pré-salé* preceded by a *ragoût de truffes* or as down-home as pig's feet and potato salad.

As African-Americans look to the 21st century, religious constraints and health concerns have given us a new dietary awareness. Yet we still revere the foods that got us through. We may not eat them every day, but the tastes of okra, corn and tomatoes, of hot sauce and hog meat, chicken and greens, remain on our tongues. They are a part of our history and a part of us all. ⌒

At my grandmothers' houses, it hadn't been called soul food, it was simply dinner.

Unknown, Woman Smiling after Completion of Peanut Crop   68

72

73

LAWRENCE DURRELL

Olives and

Orvieto

It was cold in the street
and I crossed to the lighted blaze
of shops in Rue Fuad.
In a grocer's window I saw
a small tin of olives
with the name *Orvieto* on it,
and overcome by a sudden longing to
be on the right side of the Mediterranean,
entered the shop;
bought it;
had it opened there and then;
and sitting down at a marble table
in that gruesome light
I began to eat Italy,
its dark scorched flesh,
hand-modelled spring soil,
dedicated vines.

OPPOSITE: **Sonja Bullaty & Angelo Lomeo,** Iris & Olive in Tuscany

THREE CHINESE DELICACIES

BRUCE COST

If the person who first ate an oyster was brave, what about the soul who first took a bite of what the Chinese call bird's nest — the hardened, regurgitated spittle of a swift, peppered with feathers and twigs? Even more puzzling than the fact that it was ever sampled is that, given its inaccessibility and the fuss required to prepare it, bird's nest ever caught on. And somewhere along the line, the Chinese also decided that it was worth the bother to process and eat the cartilaginous needles inside the fin of a shark. Finally, although its popularity has waxed and waned, they have long had a soft spot for the slithery, sluggish echinoderms known as holothurians, more commonly called sea slugs or sea cucumbers. **By** the beginning of the Qing Dynasty in the mid-17th century, this exotic triumvirate was standard fare for special occasions. A banquet without them was considered second-rate. It would be hard to concoct a food grouping more disparate and strange, but sea cucumber, bird's nest and shark's fin are gastronomic soul brothers, part of a large family of tasteless, gelatinous oddities for which the Chinese alone have developed an appreciation over the centuries. Other members of this family include rarities like "snow fungus" (the jellylike reproductive glands of the Beijing snow frog) as well as more common ingredients (at least to the Chinese), such as black-and-white tree fungus, duck webs, jellyfish, fish "maw" (air bladder), fish lips, the pads of bears' paws and the shin tendons of deer and beef.

If at first glance these foods seem linked only by their oddness, they constitute a category unique to Chinese cuisine. All are chewy and tasteless, depending for flavor on the food with which they are served. They are savored, by and large, for their textural

These delicacies, when dried, are thought to have a texture, an essence and a concentration of medicinal qualities...

subtleties. Beyond their exotic nature, they are distinctly similar types of high-protein gelatin that, to paraphrase the Chinese belief, "keep the bones from getting brittle," another way of saying that these foods slow the aging process. Given their common properties — fat-free protein that is, in many cases, rich in vitamins and minerals — this is not such a wacky notion. Dried jellyfish skin, for example, which is typically soaked,

parboiled and shredded for a salad, is a source of almost pure, easily digestible protein, similar to albumen, with vitamins A and B, and is reputed to lower the blood pressure.

While we in this country tend to equate health with freshness, the most highly prized and expensive of these Chinese health foods — sea cucumber, bird's nest and shark's fin, as well as tree fungus and jellyfish — are always processed by drying and are sold only in that state. These delicacies, when dried, are thought to have a texture, an essence and a concentration of medicinal qualities that make them superior to the foods in a fresh state. The difficulty of reconstituting them, particularly the three of interest here, and the skill required to prepare them only enhance their esteem. Even buying them requires the assessment of a connoisseur, especially for bird's nest and shark's fin, which, like jade, come in different grades. In recent centuries they have become status foods, often served, like fine wines, to impress guests with the host's wealth and sophistication.

One of the earliest references to the sea cucumber, or sea slug, the boneless gastronomic prize that creeps along the ocean floor, is in a document from before the 6th century. The work, called by scholars "A Canon of Gastronomy," no longer exists, although fragments of it are quoted in other contemporaneous works. At the time, the sea cucumber was called *haishu* or sea rat and it was described as "looking like a leech, but larger." Somewhere between that time and the Ming Dynasty, about a thousand years later, the creature's status was upgraded considerably and its name became *haishen* — roughly, "ginseng of the sea" — the name by which it is known today. Xia Qizhi, a 16th-century Ming writer, traced the etymology of *haishen* to the fishing folk who first harvested sea cucumbers in the North China Sea. According to the writer, they credited the sea animal with the same wondrous medicinal properties as their native ginseng.

The Chinese have harvested sea cucumbers for centuries, both along their own coasts and beyond. A thousand years ago they ventured as far as East Africa in pursuit of them. In 1415 the king of what is now Sri Lanka, annoyed at the swarms of Chinese boats fishing for sea slugs off his shore, ordered them away. According to *The Dictionary of the Economic Products of the Malay Peninsula*, the Chinese sent an army to Sri Lanka, captured the king and continued with their fishing.

Since at least the Ming period, the Chinese have culled the ocean for this creature, as far east as Fiji and south to the tropical waters off Australia. By the beginning of this century, Australian waters had been nearly fished out and in modern China, a shortage of sea cucumbers has led to soaring prices and black-market sales.

Varieties of sea slugs swim in all waters, warm or cold; they are caught off the coasts of Asia wherever the Chinese have established outposts, from Korea southward to tropical Asia and Southeast Asia. They are lethargic creatures and can be collected by scavengers wading along a coral reef at low tide, although the traditional method is for divers to moor their small boats in shallow waters and gather the sea cucumbers by hand.

Sea cucumbers are echinoderms, members of a family that includes starfish and sea urchins. After harvesting, they are doused in boiling water, slit open and eviscerated, then sun-dried to a rock-hard state and shipped to market. Before cooking, they must be soaked for several days, boiled in changes of stock or water, and cleaned. The result is a spongy, translucent seafood that, when finally cooked, has a tasteless crunch reminiscent of boiled pork fat. In spite of centuries of enjoyment, the Chinese have not managed to communicate their love for this creature much beyond their borders, although the Japanese occasionally eat them either pickled or fresh and raw as sashimi.

According to a Ming Dynasty description, the sea slug is "warming and restorative." Modern Chinese dietary experts claim that, pound for pound, sea cucumbers have almost four times the protein of beef and no cholesterol at all. But above all else, the sea cucumber's popularity rests on its supposed ability to enhance male virility. In the past, when appearances counted, great significance was attached to this phallus-shaped animal that swells at the touch. A 16th-century Chinese work reported that northern Chinese, when they couldn't get sea cucumber, "take the penis of a donkey and use it as a substitute."

Sea cucumbers are usually the featured ingredient in a dish, often cooked with other ingredients, such as pork, chicken or mushrooms, to give them flavor. A popular seafood combination, called "happy family," includes sea cucumbers along with fish maw, dried squid and other saltwater delicacies. They are also added to soups.

Preparing sea cucumbers literally takes days, and there are almost as many methods for soaking and cleaning them as there are cooks who prepare them. The goal is always a certain gelatinous resilience. One method, for those interested in the mechanics of the process, follows:

"With heat-proof tongs, hold the dried sea cucumbers over a gas flame,

In recent centuries they have become status foods, often served, like fine wines, to impress guests...

turning them from side to side, for about one minute. (They will singe slightly.) Put them into a large bowl, cover them with water and soak them overnight. Drain the next day and simmer the sea cucumbers, covered, for one and a half hours. Let them cool in their liquid, then drain and rinse them. Soak them overnight in fresh warm water once more. Drain and rinse them again. Slit open their abdomens and clean the insides, scraping with your fingernail. Simmer the sea slugs a final time in a large quantity of water with a bunch of scallions tied in a bundle and five or six slices of fresh ginger; then add them, cut in bite-sized sections if they are large, to dishes or soups."

Yuan Mei, an 18th-century Chinese gourmet and a prolific writer about food, relates an encounter with bird's nest:

"I was once asked to a party given by a certain governor, who gave us plain boiled bird's nest, served in enormous vases like flower pots. It had no taste at all. The other guests were obsequious in their praise of it. But I said, 'We are here to eat bird's nest, not to take delivery of it wholesale.' If our host's object was simply to impress, it would have been better to put a hundred pearls into each bowl. Then we should have known that the meal cost him tens of thousands, without the unpleasantness of being expected to eat what was uneatable."

The birds responsible for bird's nest are three species of swift, of the genus *Collacallia,* whose habitat ranges throughout the tropical zones of East Asia. They build their nests in colonies in huge, steep-walled caverns and in the crevices of high cliffs. Gathering them is a precarious business. Bird's nest is harvested along the coast of southern China and throughout Southeast Asia, from Vietnam to Thailand south to Indonesia and east to the Philippines. During the breeding season, the salivary glands of both male and female swifts secrete a gelatinous liquid for nest building and it is this, once hardened, that is the prize. Certain of these swifts build nests that are almost entirely saliva. Called "white nests," these are the most desirable. The top grade may be nearly complete white cups. White nests sold in pieces, called "dragon's teeth," are much less expensive

— though still no bargain. "Black nests," containing moss, feathers and grass to augment the saliva, are less esteemed, while precleaned, granular bird's nest, in varying grades, is least expensive and shunned by serious cooks.

Bird's nest is considered an elixir of the first order. Like all the gelatinous delicacies, it is thought to stave off the brittleness of age. Because the protein and other nutrients are predigested, bird's nest is considered to be especially easy on the stomach and is thought to be particularly good for the very young or very old. For all ages, it is supposed to preserve a youthful complexion and it is also prescribed for those recovering from a long illness.

Traditionally, bird's nest is not overadorned. In the classic preparation, it is served swimming in a clear, rich stock, surrounded by steamed pigeon eggs that are garnished with minced ham and coriander leaves. Also prized is a bird's-nest soup to which has been added finely minced chicken, egg white, wine and a garnish of ham. The most spectacular version I've sampled, prepared by the late master cooking teacher Virginia Lee for her students in New York, was baked in a pumpkin that had been carved and deep fried to look like an antique urn. Bird's nest is often steamed with water and rock sugar to make a sweet soup, and whether savory or sweet it is sometimes supplemented with white tree fungus or agar-agar to stretch the expensive ingredient further.

Chinese cookbooks tend to give matter-of-fact methods for preparing bird's nest, as if it were just another ingredient, like zucchini. However — and this is true for shark's fin also — bird's nest is very difficult for the home cook to make sense out of. It is helpful to have tasted different grades in the company of someone who understands it, and a brief apprenticeship with a chef who knows how to prepare it is a great help. Here is my method:

"Soak the bird's nest overnight in cold water. The next day, clean it, removing feathers and other foreign matter with tweezers. Finally, simmer it for ten minutes in stock. Drain the bird's nest, discarding the stock. Rinse the bird's nest thoroughly and squeeze it dry. A quicker method calls for soaking it for an hour in warm water, cleaning it, then soaking for five minutes in a bowl of hot water in which a little baking soda has been dissolved; the bird's nest should then be rinsed thoroughly in cold water and squeezed dry."

The term soup doesn't adequately convey the luxuriousness of a shark's-fin dish. As with bird's nest, an exquisitely rich stock is often the best medium for these clear, amber-colored, gelatinous strands that have little flavor save a hint of the sea, but shark's-fin soup may include crabmeat and crab roe. Shark's fin may also be stuffed into a duck and steamed or scrambled in eggs; and beautifully pleated shark's-fin dumpling is offered in the better *dim sum* houses. In Hong Kong, shark's-fin restaurants will list a page or more of shark's-fin dishes, with some costing hundreds of dollars for a small bowl.

A symbol of the world's most extravagant banquet fare, shark's fin is the dorsal "comb fin," or the two ventral fins, of any of a variety of sharks, most of which swim in warm Asian waters. Eating shark's fin is a relatively recent practice in Chinese food history, for it did not come into vogue until the Song Dynasty (960–1279).

While sharing the protein- and nutrient-rich properties of other delicacies, shark's fin also has status as a general tonic. It is said to "open the stomach," meaning that it is an appetite stimulator, according to the 16th-century *Bencao* or "Materia Medica." It may begin a meal or, when served at the peak of a banquet, it readies diners for the onslaught of dishes to follow.

It is not the meat that is eaten from these fins, but rather the cartilaginous needles that make up the interior. To prepare them involves an extraordinarily elaborate process of soaking and boiling in changes of water and richly seasoned stock, a chore, as a rule, not tackled by home cooks. Available at Chinese herbal shops as well as at the delicacy counter of Chinese food markets, shark's fins are typically skinned, simmered and scraped clean of most of their unwanted mucilaginous material before they come to market.

The price ranges from $40 a pound for strands, to $70 and up for the whole fin, the finest of which are dorsal fins, thick and pale yellow in color. In the most lavish presentation, the fin is served intact, traditionally wrapped for preparation in a silver net. Each chef has his or her own procedure for preparing shark's fin. The goal is to achieve a soft yet resilient texture while eliminating any fishiness. What follows is one method of many:

"Soak one pound of shark's fin, either whole or needles, in a generous amount of cold water for 24 hours, changing the water three or four times. Drain and scrub the fin as best you can with a brush. Add the fin to a wok or a large pot filled with cold water and slowly heat to boiling.

Drain and put the fin in cold water again.

When the fin has cooled, rinse it and put it in a heat-proof bowl. Heat a little peanut oil in a wok and add six scallions and a dozen slices of fresh ginger. Stir over heat until the vegetables are fragrant, then add a little Shaoxing rice wine and two cups of rich, homemade stock (chicken or, preferably, chick-

...shark's fin also has status as a general tonic.

en and duck). Bring the stock to a boil, strain it and pour it over the fin. Put the bowl with the fin and stock in a steamer and steam for three hours.

Remove the fin, discarding the cooking liquid, and carefully rinse it in three changes of hot water. It is now ready to use in most shark's fin recipes. Most simply, it can be put again into a heat-proof bowl, covered with three cups of rich chicken-duck stock that has been seasoned, including a little soy sauce for color and steamed for an hour or more. Before serving, it should be dribbled with some freshly rendered chicken fat and garnished with minced or slivered Smithfield ham." ⌒

Maryjo Koch, Sharkfin Soup 76

S. J. PERELMAN

Soda Shop of the Soul

Ah, Ye Gods of Gluttony!
That first taste, the mouthful of froth,
the sweet of the chocolate,
the brisk tang of the soda,
the ecstasy of the now-you-have-it, now-you-haven't,
which sends you on for fulfillment into the
first bite of ice cream irrigated with
the lovely fluid of the soda.

Rich though these rewards be,
they are nothing to the grand finale,
the climax of enjoyment,
when with froth gone,
ice cream gone,
you discard the straws,
lift the glass,
tilt back your head and
subject your tonsils to the first
superb shock of the pure Ichor of the soda,
syrup, bubble water, water,
melted ice cream, all blended into one
Ambrosia of flavor, action, and chill.

OPPOSITE: **Wayne Thiebaud**, Pink Swirl

A Life in Chocolate

ALICE MEDRICH

I eat chocolate every day. Sometimes people ask if I do. Some of them suspect addiction. Others are probably happy to find a kindred spirit. I don't feel defensive about it. So I do not feel compelled to add that on most days the chocolate that I eat is only a tiny taste — because that is all that is necessary .... On most days. **I** grew up on chocolate, American-style. I liked the shiny dark layer of skin, slightly chewy, on top of Royal Chocolate Pudding. Chocolate bars were treats, not junk food. My Dad bought Hershey Bars from the snack bar at the drive-in (I grew up in L.A.) and tossed them in our laps as he climbed back into the car. We unveiled and nibbled them, each with our own private ritual — breaking off and carefully rationing each tiny square or chomping right into the whole bar. Even today, tearing a wrapper and breathing the mingling smells of foil and chocolate instantly transports me back in time. **On** warm evenings in Southern California in the 50s, we'd drive 20 minutes to get a chocolate ice cream cone or soda. Not because the nearest or best chocolate ice cream was 20 minutes away, rather because a drive was a family outing in those days. We managed to enjoy each other and sustain good behavior long enough to reach the promised chocolate ice cream. My mother taught us how to order a chocolate soda properly, with chocolate ice cream. I still do it that way. I also buy enough Milky Ways at Halloween to ensure frozen leftovers – we ate Milky Ways directly from the freezer.

Comfort food? Never mind meatloaf and mashed potatoes, I think first of chocolate. At a moment of personal crisis in college, a friend I'd known well since the third grade took me for a hot fudge sundae. It was not a frivolous gesture, it was a gift of momentary distraction from painful decisions. Years

My mother taught us how to order a chocolate soda properly, with chocolate ice cream...we ate Milky Ways directly from the freezer.

later, when I had a miscarriage, another friend grabbed a chocolate ice cream bar from her freezer – to console me. I remember both occasions clearly – and the thick dark chocolate at the bottom of the sundae glass and the cold frosty Fudgesicle against my teeth. But most of all, I remember the care of true and knowing friends.

It is assumed, because of my professional relationship to chocolate, as an author and as founding chef of Cocolat, that somewhere along the way I saw the light, grew up, turned away from childhood chocolate and became sophisticated and refined, only eating the best dark chocolate. It is assumed that I evaluate every chocolate dessert I encounter. A long time ago people stopped making chocolate desserts if I was going to be a guest (too bad). The fact is, I do have an educated palate and I adore some of the truly fine and highly touted chocolates. But that does not cancel a lifelong love affair with chocolate – or do justice to the nature of chocolate or the powerful roll of context and memory, comfort and reward.

When I was 22 my husband, Elliott, took the post-doctoral dream job – one year in Paris. In the fall of 1973 we moved into an eccentric two-room flat in the 16th arrondissement. Our landlady (also eccentric) presented us with homemade chocolate truffles for the first time on my husband's birthday, then on mine and later at Christmas (by which time she had recruited me to help form and roll them in cocoa). One bite of Madame Lestelle's cocoa-dusted chocolate truffle suggested a world beyond the chocolate I knew: Smooth, dense, earthy and bittersweet – a jolt of pure chocolate poetry. It was not the aching sweetness of a piece of fudge or the cloying comfort of a Hershey's Kiss. It was a sensual pleasure like elegant slightly erotic prose compared to a frilly valentine. A swoon instead of a giggle.

That year in Paris was filled with astonishment – until then I didn't know a tomato could explode on your tongue with sweet acidity, that a peach could fill the room and your senses with edible fragrance or that fois gras was like nothing else in the world. And oh, the chocolate desserts! The best nibbling-quality chocolate was lavished on those desserts. Chocolate for grownups – smooth and subtle, yet intensely chocolate without excessive sweetness. I sought flourless chocolate tortes, chased souffle cakes, admired mousses and hunted treasured truffles. Ganache entered my life and lexicon.

How could the liaison between fresh cream and good chocolate be compared to ordinary chocolate candy? In our tiny oven with no thermostat on the Rue Copernic, I managed a simple but heavenly chocolate cake. I remember what I was wearing and where I was standing when I tasted it. Even though it's been 20 years!

An infusion of European ideas, recipes and chocolate sparked a renaissance. Chocolate in America got better! Our beloved brownies, devil's food and hot fudge sundaes were revisited or reinterpreted and very often made with better chocolate than ever before. They now mingle on menus with mousse au chocolat and the now ubiquitous flourless chocolate torte.

The fallout from raised chocolate consciousness? The inevitable quest for The Ultimate. I am constantly asked which chocolate is best. Indeed, we (in the chocolate community) hold endless blind tastings and comparisons. Each time I participate in a tasting I get excited by the opportunity to taste the differences (although I agonize terribly over ranking them).

Once I tasted eleven chocolates ranging in style and varietal character and sweetness. Some stood out with characteristics such as smokiness, winey flavor, extra dark cocoa-y taste or a little more sweetness. These chocolates tended to be ranked either at the top or bottom of the list. Is smoky good or bad?

The more I taste, the more obvious it is that responses are subjective, colored by individual histories and palates — and mostly heedless of the formal criteria established by experts. Does it matter if the tasting panel is from one region of the country versus another? Does familiarity breed contempt or fondness (what did your family nibble at the movies)?

Generally I prefer assertive flavors. I appreciate acidity and bitterness in foods (strong coffee, astringent salad dressing, lots of lemon, strong cheeses, dry flinty white wines). My chocolate preferences differ from those of someone who prefers sweeter softer flavors and subtler milder foods. Texture affects some people's perception of flavor more than others'. Often I have noticed that a chocolate that is extra smooth and creamy on the palate — but otherwise ordinary tasting — will rank high with a panel of tasters. Chocolate with a hard crisp snap and exceptional flavor may be dismissed as waxy — despite the fact that professionals regard crisp snap as a sign of quality.

The formal tasting process is imperfect. It doesn't tell me which chocolate is The Best or even which chocolate I like the best. But the process is infinitely fascinating. It places an array of tastes and textures before me like colors on an artist's palette and reminds me that chocolate, like wine and coffee and cheese and all of the other foods that I love, is rich with complexities.

Leftovers from a tasting illustrate my point. After all the tasters have gone home and absent the pressure of having to evaluate and rank the samples, there is nothing left but to enjoy. After one great tasting I had lots left over.

Every day I chose a taste. One evening after dinner I chose a very refined and elegant nibble with exotic varietal cocoa flavors. The next day I was in the mood for something more robust. A guest enjoyed one of the milder chocolates. If someone dropped by, I put out small tastes of two or three chocolates.

A chocolate that makes a superlative brownie

A jolt of pure chocolate poetry ...A swoon instead of a giggle.

may not be the same chocolate that makes a magnificent mousse or the best midnight snack. Time, place, mood and company add endless permutations to the experience. (Who wants the same thing every day?) The search is infinitely rewarding, but I would never really want to find the mythical "best" chocolate.

Once in a while I still buy and enjoy a Hershey Bar at the movies or slip a Nestle's Crunch into my bag at the airport. None of this affects the exquisite pleasure of a tiny piece of Valrhona chocolate next to my espresso cup in a Paris café or that moment of bittersweet heaven when I encounter a perfect chocolate truffle. ⌒

Michael Lamotte, Brownie and Glass of Milk 84

KHANH VO DANG

(9½ Years Old)

Ice Cream

Pizza

The rain of heart

The sun of vanilla

I'm as crazy as a street

My eyes shine

The rainbows flash

The ice cream pizza

The snowy turtle

The red, black, orange moon

Pizza soup

The baby mask

The vanilla car

The heart of writing

Star heart

Blue star running

The hand of ocean light

The gold of shark

The gold of zebra

The heart of ocean

The sun of piranha

The sky of rainbow

The heart of moon

The sun turtle

The rising horse

The talking of sun

The music of sound

Music of heart

Star lion

Ocean lion ice cream

The piranha of vanilla

OPPOSITE: **Ann Arnold,** Ice Cream Pizza

THE LANGUAGES OF WINE

ALBERT SONNENFELD

"Wine is bottled poetry," rhapsodized Robert Louis Stevenson in *The Silverado Squatters.* The poetry of "these imperial elixirs, beautiful to every sense, gem-hued, flower-scented, dream-compellers" contains and reveals the secret memories of the soil. Colette, that supreme sensualist, wrote lyrically that "even flint can be living, yielding, nourishing. Even the unemotional chalk weeps in wine, golden tears." Like the painting that stands revealed only when there is a beholder, like the unheard melody that expresses its true sweetness only when sung, the poetry held in suspension within the bottle must be released, like a genie; to "exist" the wine must be unbottled and tasted. **But** wine requires a further step for its poetry to be fully sensed and communicated. Wine must be commented upon, discussed, debated. Reflection, it has been said by Pierre Poupon, must follow reflex; idea follows the sensation. **In** France, a coarse red wine becomes *"l'absinthe de vidangeur"* (roto-rooter absinthe). For a velvety smooth Cabernet, countryfolk in the Bordelais say: *"C'est le petit Jésus qui vous descend dans le gosier en culottes de velours"*

("It's baby Jesus in velvet pants going down your gullet"). That charming French encomium may not be high poetry; it is a poetry of wine, nonetheless, communicating tactile velvety smoothness as well as reminding us of the sacramental nature of wine from Dionysus to the Wedding at Cana. That religious centrality was reflected in a rare ecumenical drink shared by priest and rabbi. When the rabbi watered his Beaujolais the priest said, "I see you baptize your wine." "No," answered the rabbi circumspectly, "I cut it."

Drinking wine is not a solitary pleasure. Bartles had to tell Jaymes of the sugar-infested glories of their "cooler;" the word *symposium,* as in Plato's *Symposium,* etymologically means "drinking together," "a drinking, conversation and intellectual entertainment," which describes many an academic meeting. In Plato's work, wine is forbidden to 18-year-olds, but after age 40 it is virtually prescription medicine, making us kinder, gentler, tempering our passions "as fire softens iron, giving health to the soul." No wonder the French call it *"le lait des vieillards"* (old men's milk)!

To state that the modern "languages of wine" grew first in French soil is not egregious snobbery but ecological, historical and religious fact: There is the importance of a centralized court culture, to be sure, and the symbolically focused role of wine in Catholic liturgy cannot be overstated. In contrast, in America, there was Prohibition but, above all, the lingering vestiges of centuries of Cromwellian Puritanism, which impede Anglo-Saxon wine culture even today. Why do British pubs have leaded windows hiding the drinkers from the condemning gaze of the passer-by, whereas the French and Italians drink openly and contentedly on sidewalk terraces?

The great poet of wine, Charles Baudelaire, once wrote that "a man who drinks only water must be hiding a shameful secret from his fellow-men." It is a too little-known fact that in the U.S.A. wine comes under the control of the Bureau of Alcohol, Tobacco and Firearms, and that recently the Bureau refused to allow Kermit Lynch to quote on his wine label Founding Father Thomas Jefferson's testimony that "Wine from long habit has become an indispensable for my health." The ruling, a masterful piece of bureaucratic gobbledygook, is well worth reading:

"A statement that attributes positive health benefits to the moderate consumption of wine, *even if backed up by medical evidence* [italics mine], may have an overall misleading effect, if such statement is not properly qualified, does not give both sides of the issue, and does not outline the categories of individuals for whom such positive effect would be outweighed by numerous negative health effects."

In French a wine label is an *étiquette,* the same word that describes the decorum of drinking and discussing wine. One of the 19th-century pioneers of Napa Valley wine, the Hungarian emigrant A. Haraszthy, labeled the average American of his time a "whisky-drinking, water-drinking, coffee-drinking and consequently dyspepsia-inviting subject .... The task before us [he continued] lies in teaching our people how to drink wine, when to drink it, and how much of it to drink." He might have added: how to talk the languages of wine.

> **"The task before us...lies in teaching our people how to drink wine, when to drink it, and how much of it to drink."**

A British Victorian poet put it this way:

"The French have taste in all they do
Which we are quite without
For Nature that to them gave *goût*
To us gave only gout."
– Erskine, *1850*

That may be too self-deprecatory for a compatriot of Ruskin's. While not wishing to privilege French wine, I cannot deny that the languages of wine derive from the French linguistic tradition and constitute one indispensable facet of that tradition's immortality.

We have all, I am sure, been irritated by an inflated poetry of wine ridiculed perfectly in the famous 1937 *New Yorker* cartoon by James Thurber, presenting "a naive domestic Burgundy without any breeding, but I think you'll be amused by its presumption." Even such often comical pretensions and preciosity embody the poetic processes of simile, analogy and personification. Thus, a Frenchman can "see a wine's bones" (*On lui voit les os*), or "feel its flesh" (*bien nourri, charnu*). Wine can be "young, timid" (*jeune, jeunet*) or "old, tired, senile, dead" (*décrépit, sénile, claqué*). If Charles Monselet called Bordeaux "feminine" and Burgundy "masculine," many oenophiles would reverse those gender labels because of Bordeaux's greater tannin and astringency. Nonetheless, wine is treated linguistically as feminine, and drinking it is an erotic act. Wine "has a navel" (*il a du nombril*), "thighs" (*de la cuisse*). To open a bottle is "to deflower it" (*la dépuceler*), to drink the wine is "to caress it" (*la caresser*) and to down a whole bottle of the dark vin de Cahors is "to strangle" or "suffocate a Negress" (*étrangler, étouffer une Négresse*). For an excitable barfly a strong non-vintage red is "a thigh-opener" (*un ouvre-cuisses*).

To be sure, this picturesque traditional language of wine is sexist in the extreme, and one wonders at times whether our intention is to drink the wine or to marry it. There is an excess of machismo in the imagery of drinking: "grease your wheels" (*se graisser les roues*), "fill up with fuel, anti-skid, anti-freeze" (*faire le plein de carburant, antidérapant, antigel*). What is happening in these picturesque locutions is not mere verbal juggling, however. The popular imagination is trying, verbally, to express the inexpressible, the ineffable mystery of taste and smell. Even in classical wine language, to describe a perfume or a taste one has, perforce, to have recourse to analogy, evoking resemblance to a flower, to a fruit, spice or food. Hence, the usual wine vocabulary of our

journalist. A Château Léoville-Lascases 1971 has "intense color, a nuanced bouquet, fruity, spicy, truffled with vanilla"; a 1967 Château Grand-Barrail Lamarzelle-Figeac has "a well-developed bouquet, difficult to analyze, with echoes of very ripe fruit, woods, venison, and an aroma of cocoa."

If what the eye sees, the "robe" or color and the "aspect" or clarity of a wine, are relatively concrete and easy to verbalize, the much more elusive and inextricably entwined senses of smell and taste would seem to authorize the wildest excesses of verbal extravagance and synesthesia. We breathe and smell the wine both directly through the nose and through the back of the mouth (retronasally), the famous *"arôme de bouche."* What can we then say that would be worthy of this now "unbottled poetry?" We must find what would seem to be a subjective analogy: that a 1967 Nuits-Saint-Georges Perrières has a "bouquet of cassis-raspberry-vanilla with a discreet touch of fine wood." In fact, describing wine bouquet is much less subjective than, say, characterizing women's perfumes. How do we "communicate" Lanvin's *Arpège*, to what do we compare it? A perfume's name is always chosen as total metaphor: *Arpège, Opium, Obsession.*

What can we then say that would be worthy of this now "unbottled poetry?"

Scientists, from the 18th-century Linnaeus to our contemporary Jean Lenoir (in *Le Nez du Vin*) have sought to classify smells and have come up with 10 basic categories: animal, balsamic, woodsy, chemical, spicy or aromatic, fire or burned, fermented or etherized, floral, fruity, vegetal. The scientific aspect of oenology results from laboratory experiments: Chemists have analyzed the volatiles in wines and have discovered that the analogies perceived by the most expert noses among us are in chemical fact present. So that in the laboratory, a 1955 Pauillac Lynch-Bages might now be described as "exuding a bouquet of acetate d'isoamyle, of phenlylethylic acid, with touches of glycyrryzine and benzaldehyde cyanhydrine." Or, in short, "a complex bouquet of banana, of honey, with touches of anise and cherry." Clearly, such chemical precision, however surreal and high-tech its glacially scientific poetry, does not make for graceful table-talk among oenophiles!

Great wines are "texts," and tasting wine is "reading" the wine, parsing out its syllables, its hieroglyphs, as we move through the some 30 seconds from attack to evolution to finale, sorting out the sugars, acids and bitters as they interact. Then we speak, each in his

own way, in the many languages of wine; the apparently affected, the scientific, the popular.

Charles Baudelaire, who called wine *"le fils sacré du soleil"* (the holy off-spring of the sun), addressed those who, like himself, sought in wine to remember or to forget. Those who drink to forget are too numerous still: There are 278 terms for wine-induced drunkenness in contemporary French alone. The escapist clientele is revealed by its language: "drunk and armored as a tank, an aircraft carrier, the Siegfried line." If red wine is (or used to be) "Soviet whiskey," one can (in French) be "drunk as an Englishman, a Pole, a duck, a turkey, a tick and a cow."

As early as 1580, Montaigne complained that Germans swallow rather than taste. But those, it is often noted, who seek to forget, or who drink for aphrodisiac effect, inevitably turn to stronger brew. Or as Ernest Dowson put it charmingly: "Absinthe makes the tart grow fonder."

I prefer to see as symbolic of America's oenological growth and evolving taste that the legendary gin-drinker, Ernest Hemingway, should have a granddaughter named Margaux! While we may be disturbed that all the statistical evidence – even from France – tells us that people are now drinking less wine, it should be reemphasized that they are drinking better; and fine wines, insisted Emile Peynaud, lead to sobriety. For Rabelais, the great Renaissance drinker from Chinon, the sacred bottle (*La Dive Bouteille*) is full of all mystery and contains all truth. Wine, in French as in English, rhymes with divine (*vin/divin*). "Taste memory, the ability to recall a taste sensation," James Beard wrote, "is a God-given talent, akin to perfect pitch, which makes your life richer." We may not all have been blessed by God with that talent, but we can all join the Symposium (the drinking together) to honor Dionysus. Let us not forget that when the Vikings discovered the New World they called it "Vineland." As one ecologist put it recently: "Wine is by far the best use for solar energy." And each Autumn we can celebrate with the poet John Keats that

"Season of the mists and mellow fruitfulness,
Close-bosom friend of the maturing sun;
Conspiring with him how to load and bless
With fruit the vines …."

From its very beginning in the gloriously secular Age of Enlightenment, the 18th century, our country has had prominent spokesmen for the cause of wine. In 1791 Thomas Jefferson wrote:

"I rejoice as a moralist at the prospect of a reduction of duties on wine by our national legislature. It is an error to view a tax on that

Great wines are "texts," and tasting wine is "reading" the wine, parsing out its syllables, its hieroglyphs, as we move through the some 30 seconds from attack to evolution to finale...

liquor as merely a tax on the rich …. No nation is drunken where wine is cheap; and none sober where the dearness of wine substitutes ardent spirits as the common beverage. [Wine] is, in truth, the only antidote to the bane of whiskey."

Strong words that should be heeded; but let us end on a less sobering note, these comforting words by Benjamin Franklin: "Wine is a constant proof that God loves us and loves to see us happy."

94
95

Michelangelo Caravaggio,
Young Bacchus   90

Bartolomeo Bimbi,
Grapes of 38 Varieties (detail)   94

ART & TEXT CREDITS

ART

COVER AND PAGE 101
Thomas Heinser, Robert Mondavi
Holding Grapes, photographed for
The AIWF, © 1996 Thomas Heinser,
San Francisco, CA

FRONTISPIECE
Giuseppe Arcimboldo, Autumn, 1573,
Louvre, Erich Lessing/Art Resource, NY

PAGES X–XI, 94
Bartolomeo Bimbi, Grapes of 38
Varieties, Palazzo Pitti, Florence,
Scala/Art Resource, NY

PAGE 2
Dante Gabriel Rossetti, Proserpine,
1874, Tate Gallery, London, Bridgeman
Art Library

PAGE 7
Dante Gabriel Rossetti, Day Dream,
1880, Victoria & Albert Museum,
London, Bridgeman Art Library

PAGE 8
Reinhart Wolf, Piglet, The Stockmarket

PAGE 10-11
Reinhart Wolf, Eggs, The Stockmarket

PAGE 12
Reinhart Wolf, Chinese Farmer, The
Stockmarket

PAGE 13
Reinhart Wolf, Woman and Chestnuts,
The Stockmarket

PAGE 14
Unknown, Colette dans son Jardin à
St. Sauveur-En-Puisaye, Collèction
Roger-Viollet, Paris, © Harlingue-Viollet

PAGE 21
Unknown, Colette Willy, Collèction
Roger-Viollet, Paris, © Harlingue-Viollet

PAGE 22
Connor Leech, Crazy Grape, 1996
Mill Valley, CA

PAGE 23
Lily Guy, Grapes on the Vine, 1996,
Belvedere, CA

PAGES 24-25
James Burke, Green Grapes on a Plate,
1996, Belvedere, CA

Sophie Anna Greenberg,
Oh!… Splash!, 1996, Tiburon, CA

Connor Leech, Grapes in Hawaii, 1996,
Mill Valley, CA

Elisabeth Wilkie, Checkered Grapes,
1996, Mill Valley, CA

PAGE 26
Carole P. Meredith, Pinot Noir
Grapes, Dept. of Viticulture & Enology,
University of California, Davis, CA

PAGE 31
Luca Forte, Still Life, 18th century,
Agnew & Sons, London, Bridgeman
Art Library

PAGE 32
Henri Matisse, Tulips and Oysters on a
Black Background, 1943, Musée Picasso,
Paris, © Succession H. Matisse/Artists
Rights Society, New York, NY, Courtesy
Réunion des Musées Nationaux

PAGE 34
Jonathan Koch, Ultra Low-Fat Cook,
1996, Santa Cruz, CA

PAGE 38-39
Jacopo Palma Vecchio, The Three
Sisters, 1520-25, Gemaeldegalerie,
Staatliche Kunstsammlungen, Dresden,
Germany, Erich Lessing/Art Resource, NY

PAGE 42
William H. Johnson, Still Life with
Onions, Jug, and Fruit, National Museum
of American Art, Washington, DC/
Art Resource, NY

PAGE 44
Unknown, Painting from the tomb of
Nebamun,18th dynasty, British Museum,
London,Werner Forman Archive/
Art Resource, NY

PAGE 48
Elizabeth Rice, Apples and Pears, 20th
century, Private Collection, Bridgeman
Art Library

PAGE 50
Elizabeth Rice, Potato, Aubergine and
Winter Cherry, 20th century, Private
Collection, Bridgeman Art Library

PAGE 51
Elizabeth Rice, Onions and Other
Vegetables, 20th century, Private
Collection, Bridgeman Art Library

PAGE 52
Gary Kelley, Hard Scrabble Farmer,
Darien, CT

PAGE 63
Gary Kelley, Farmscape, Darien, CT

PAGE 64
Vivienne Flesher, Neruda's Wine
Glass, Pt. Reyes Station, CA

PAGE 68
Unknown, Woman Smiling after
Completion of Peanut Crop, 1870,
The Bettmann Archive

PAGE 74
Sonja Bullaty & Angelo Lomeo,
Iris & Olive in Tuscany, © 1994 Sonja
Bullaty & Angelo Lomeo, New York, NY

PAGE 76
Maryjo Koch, Sharkfin Soup, 1996,
Santa Cruz, CA

PAGE 82
Wayne Thiebaud, Pink Swirl,
20th century, Alan Stone Galleries,
New York, NY

PAGE 84
Michael Lamotte, Brownie and Glass
of Milk, San Francisco, CA

PAGE 88
Ann Arnold, Ice Cream Pizza, 1996,
Berkeley, CA

PAGE 90
Michelangelo Caravaggio, Young
Bacchus, Uffizi, Florence, Scala/Art
Resource, NY

TEXT

PAGE IX
R.W. Apple Jr., written and
presented as a salute to Robert
Mondavi at The AIWF Rare Wine
Auction, 1994

PAGE 3-6
Diane Ackerman, "The Bloom of the
Taste Bud," from A Natural History of the
Senses, Copyright © 1990 by Diane
Ackerman. Reprinted by permission of
Random House, Inc.

PAGES 15-21
Alice Wooledge Salmon, "Colette and
Wine," The Journal of Gastornomy, Vol. I,
no. 3, The American Institute of Wine &
Food, Winter, 1985

PAGES 27-30
Marq De Villiers, selected excerpt
from The Heartbreak Grape, Copyright
© 1994 by Jacobus Communications
Corp. Reprinted by permission of
HarperCollins Publishers, Inc.

PAGE 33
Anne Sexton, "Oysters," from
The Book of Folly, Copyright © 1972 by
Anne Sexton. Reprinted by permission of
Houghton Mifflin Co. All rights reserved.

PAGES 35-41
Jeffrey Steingarten, selected excerpt
from "In the Low-Fat Kitchen," Vogue,
April, 1995

PAGE 43
Adrienne Rich, "Peeling Onions,"
from Collected Early Poems: 1950-1970 by
Adrienne Rich. Copyright © 1993,
1963 by Adrienne Rich. Reprinted by
permission of the author and W.W.
Norton & Company, Inc.

PAGES 45-47
R.W. Apple Jr., "Innard Beauty," Saveur,
No 9, Nov./Dec., 1995

PAGES 53-62
Will Weaver, "The Gleaners,"
The Journal of Gastronomy, Vol. 5, no. 2,
The American Institute of Wine & Food,
Summer/Autumn, 1989

PAGES 65-67
Pablo Neruda, "Ode to Wine,"
Selected Odes of Pablo Neruda, University
of California Press, 1990

PAGES 69-73
Jessica B. Harris, an excerpt from
The Welcome Table, Copyright © 1995
by Jessica B. Harris. Reprinted with the
permission of Simon & Schuster

PAGE 75
Lawrence Durrell, an excerpt from
Justine, Dutton, 1957

PAGES 77-81
Bruce Cost, "Three Chinese Delicacies:
Sea Cucumber, Bird's Nest, Shark's Fin,"
The Journal of Gastronomy, Vol. 3, no. 3,
The American Institute of Wine & Food,
Autumn, 1987

PAGE 83
S.J. Perelman, an excerpt from The
Road to Milltown or Under the Spreading
Atrophy, Simon & Schuster, 1957

PAGES 85-87
Alice Medrich, "A Life in Chocolate,"
Au Juice: The Journal of Eatin' Drinkin' &
Screwin' 'Round, No. 2, December, 1995.

PAGE 89
Khanh Vo Dang, "Ice Cream Pizza,"
created during a workshop with
California Poets in the Schools, 1995

PAGES 91-95
Albert Sonnenfeld, "The Languages
of Wine," presented at The AIWF
1991 Conference on Gastronomy, The
French American Review, Vol. 64, no. 2,
Winter, 1993

Wine and food, as the oldest of humankind's arts, are at the heart of how a nation or a culture defines civilization. That those arts should have come of age in the last three decades in America is cause for celebration and exploration.

That is the mission of The American Center For Wine, Food And The Arts: to explore, integrate and celebrate wine and food in relation to the other arts in expressing and creating our uniquely American way of life.

On 13 acres along the Napa River, work will begin in the spring of 1997 on a facility that integrates galleries and lecture rooms, theaters and amphitheaters, kitchens and vineyards, libraries and gardens in a setting of sunshine and water surrounded by rolling hills.

In this happy climate, The Center will bring together winemakers, chefs, scholars, artists and craftspeople to provide an innovative educational center for future leaders in these fields and for the general public. In its central location, The Center will further the educational and research programs both of the University of California at Davis and of The American Institute of Wine & Food, for which it will provide new headquarters.

The Center will foster experimental programs in viticulture and culinary education and will create a multi-disciplinary forum for studying the politics of food, diet and health, sustainable agriculture and food supply. It will create traveling exhibitions, seminars, publications and a permanent multimedia library. The Center's outdoor and indoor theaters will showcase performances of music, drama and the dance to enlarge the context of the arts of wine and food.

Thirty years ago, Robert Mondavi dreamed of producing wines in Napa Valley that might join the great wines of the world. Today, the fulfillment of that dream is the rock on which The Center will stand to proclaim that American wine and American food occupy a place of honor on the world's map.

Believing that knowledge of food and drink is essential to the quality of human life, the founders of The American Institute of Wine & Food – Julia Child, Robert Mondavi and Richard Graff – 15 years ago created a nonprofit educational organization with membership open to all. Currently, The AIWF has over 9,000 individual members and a total of 34 chapters in North America and France.

By bringing food and wine professionals together with dedicated enthusiasts, The AIWF provides a unique forum for increasing our understanding and appreciation of food and drink through a lively series of conferences, publications and chapter programs. Members have a chance to exchange ideas with experts of many kinds, from chefs, restaurateurs, marketers and winemakers to journalists, physicians, anthropologists and artists.

Since education is the core of The AIWF, the organization works with many universities, national organizations, agencies and individuals to develop particular programs. The AIWF's ongoing programs include: the Annual International Conference on Gastronomy; Taste & Health (which brings together health and taste professionals); the Taste Curriculum for Schoolchildren; Workshops on Biotechnology; and a series of programs to explore the impact of the world's gastronomic cultures on our own.

An important library resource is The AIWF National Collection on Gastronomy, housed both at the Schlesinger Library of Radcliffe College and at the Mandeville Special Collections Library of the University of California at San Diego.

Local programs feature tastings, culinary tours, educational events and work to foster direct links between local farmers and consumers in many kinds of marketplaces.

Diane Ackerman (*A Natural History of the Senses; The Natural History of Love; The Moon by Whale Light; Jaguar of Sweet Laughter: New and Selected Poems*) is a frequent contributor to *The New Yorker* and lives in upstate New York.

R.W. Apple Jr. (*Apple's Europe*) is Washington bureau chief of *The New York Times,* where he writes on national politics, foreign policy and economic issues. Since joining the *Times* in 1963, he has served as bureau chief in Saigon, Lagos, Nairobi, London and Moscow. Mr. Apple appears frequently on national television and is a former member of The AIWF national board of directors.

Bruce Cost (*Ginger East to West; Asian Ingredients*), a chef and caterer, studied Chinese cookery with the late Virginia Lee. He lives in San Francisco, California.

Marq De Villiers (*Down the Volga in a Time of Troubles; The Heartbreak Grape; White Tribe Dreaming*) is a veteran journalist, editor and publisher who lives in Toronto and Lunenberg, Nova Scotia.

Lawrence Durrell (*Alexandria Quartet; Justine; Bitter Lemons*), born a British citizen in the Himalaya region of India in 1912, wrote and traveled until his death in 1990.

Jessica B. Harris (*Tasting Brazil; Iron Pots and Wooden Spoons; Sky Juice and Flying Fish*) lives in Brooklyn, New York, is a professor at Queens College and lectures at numerous institutions. Her articles have appeared in *Eating Well, Food & Wine, Essence* and *The New Yorker.* She is a current member of the AIWF national board of directors.

Mar West Studio, an art studio in Tiburon, California, was founded by Annelies Atchley. The work of several of her young students was featured in "American Children: Art of The Grape." Atchley has taught children, seniors and youths through local schools and in her workshops since 1964.

Alice Medrich (*Cocolat: Extraordinary Chocolate Desserts; Chocolate and the Art of Low-Fat Desserts*) of Berkeley, California, received formal training at École Lenôtre outside Paris. She has won numerous culinary honors, including the Wine and Food Achievement Award in 1991.

Pablo Neruda (*Book of Questions; Odes to Common Things; 100 Love Sonnets; Ceremonial Songs*) was born in 1904 in Parral, Chile, and died in 1973 in Santiago. Among his many books were four volumes of odes to ordinary people, places, things and events, published between 1954 and 1959. In 1971, Neruda was awarded the Nobel Prize for Literature.

S.J. Perelman (*The Road to Milltown or Under the Spreading Atrophy*) developed his own genre of wit, idiosyncratic vocabulary, punning titles, intricate rhetorical devices and adventurous sentence structure. He lived from 1904 to 1979, mostly in New York.

Adrienne Rich (*A Wild Patience Has Taken Me This Far; Blood, Bread, and Poetry; An Atlas of the Difficult World*) graduated from Radcliffe in 1951, the same year she published her first volume of poetry. She has received two Guggenheim Fellowships and has taught at Swarthmore College, Columbia University and Brandeis University. She lives in Santa Cruz, California.

Alice Wooledge Salmon (*Cooking With Style*) is a native of New York City, a graduate of Vassar and a resident of London. Her work has appeared in the British and American editions of *House & Garden* as well as in *Gourmet,* British *Vogue, Stand, Convivium, The World of Interiors, Food and Wine* and elsewhere. She has twice won the Glenfiddich Award for Food Writer of the Year and is currently writing a series of short stories.

Anne Sexton (*To Bedlam and Part Way Back; Transformations; Mercy Street*) spearheaded the confessional poetry movement of the 1960s. A student of Robert Lowell and a contemporary of Sylvia Plath, she taught at Boston University and Colgate. She won the 1966 Pulitzer Prize for her collection *Live or Die.* Sexton died in 1974.

Albert Sonnenfeld, professor and chair of the Department of French and Italian at the University of Southern California, is also an essayist, editor, lecturer and raconteur on subjects ranging from Proust to petits fours. He lives in Brentwood, California. Mr. Sonnenfeld is a former member of the AIWF national board of directors.

Jeffrey Steingarten is a lawyer by training. He is the Food Editor of *Vogue* magazine and a prize-winning journalist. Steingarten lives in New York City.

Khanh Vo Dang is a student at Maxwell Elementary School in Oakland, California. He wrote his poem during a workshop brought to his class by California Poets in the Schools, a San Francisco-based poetry education program.

Will Weaver (*Red Earth, White Earth; Striking Out; A Gravestone Made of Wheat*) has won prizes from the McKnight and Bush foundations, The National Endowment for the Arts and the PEN Fiction Project. He lives in Bemidji, Minnesota.